The Babylonian Captivity of the Mainline Church

The Babylonian Captivity of the Mainline Church

Charles H. Bayer

Chalice Press
St. Louis, Missouri

© Copyright 1996 by Charles H. Bayer.

All rights reserved. No part of this book may be reproduced without written permission from Chalice Press, P.O. Box 179, St. Louis, MO 63166-0179.

Biblical quotations, unless otherwise noted, are from the *New Revised Standard Version Bible*, copyright 1989, Division of Christian Education of the National Council of the Churches of Christ in the USA. Used by permission.

Design: Lynne Condellone
Cover design/art direction: Michael Domínguez

10 9 8 7 6 5 4 3 2 1   96 97 98 99 00 01

*Dedicated to
Carol, Beth, Jenni, Mary, and Sean.
May they learn to love the church.*

Library of Congress Cataloging–in–Publication Data

Bayer, Charles H.
    The Babylonian captivity of the mainline church / Charles H. Bayer.
       p.   cm.
   ISBN 0-8272-0221-0
    1. Liberalism (Religion)—Protestant churches—History—20th century.   2. Liberalism (Religion)—United States—History—20th century.   3. Liberalism (Religion)—Protestant churches—Forecasting.   4. Liberalism (Religion)—United States—Forecasting.   5. United States—Church history—20th century.   I. Title.
BR526.B388   1996
280'.4'097309045—dc20   95-50674
                                                                                CIP
                         Printed in the United States of America

Contents

	Preface	vii
1	The Captivity	1
2	How Shall the Mainline Church Respond?	15
3	Staying Authentic Today While Preparing for Tomorrow	29
4	The Theological Imperative and the Work of the Minister	46
5	The Nature of Faith: From Theology to Praxis	59
6	Shaping a Community of Learners	76
7	Spiritual Formation and the Worshiping Community	92
8	Evangelism and Social Witness	111
9	The Communion of Saints	130
10	Are Denominations Out of Date?	141
11	Ecumenism and a Church in Exile	161
12	"Love the Church!"	171

Preface

This book has grown out of a lifelong lover's quarrel with the church. I believe it to be one of God's best hopes for this troubled world. Over a forty-year ministry I have courted her, wedded her, fought with her, rediscovered her, and prayed unceasingly for her.

Wendy, my wife, is my most dedicated and enthusiastic fan. A testimony to her devotion came when, after hearing one of Fred Craddock's best sermons (which is just about any sermon Fred preaches), she exclaimed, "Why, he's even better than you are!" (Whereupon a nearby colleague remarked, "He's even better than you *think* you are!") Wendy's careful reading and modifying of the text were enormously helpful. In the coming year we will set out together on a new venture as we have been jointly appointed by the Christian Church (Disciples of Christ) and the United Church of Christ to teach at the Churches of Christ Theological College in Mulgrave, Australia.

Michael Kinnamon, dean of Lexington Theological Seminary, and other members of that faculty were gracious in critiquing two of the chapters presented in revised form as the 1995 Stauffer Lectures there. David Polk, of Chalice Press, who has both edited and encouraged the writing of this book, deserves a world of thanks, as do the congregations of First Christian Church, St. Joseph, Missouri, and University Church of Chicago, Illinois. The long and faithful journeys of these two congregations have provided most of the positive examples of what churches ought to be, and can be.

Charles Bayer
St. Joseph, Missouri

1 | The Captivity

As we stand on the cusp of a new millennium, the historic Protestant church is languishing in what may be the first years of a new Babylonian captivity. This book attempts to come to terms with how a people of faith sing the Lord's songs in this strange land. If at one time the churches whose life flowed from the Reformation—European and English—were considered mainline, they are now clearly sideline. If once they set the religious agenda in the United States, as well as in much of Western Europe and its empires, they are now increasingly ignored. On one hand, an energetic secularism pays them scant attention; on the other hand, an equally energetic fundamentalist-charismatic-evangelical wave has taken the center of the religious stage.

When the secular world wants to know what the Christian position is on any one of a variety of issues, members of the former mainline churches are rarely presented with the interrogatories. Two generations ago, names such as Tillich, Barth, Niebuhr, Fosdick, and Brunner were part of the working vocabulary of significant numbers of America's laity. Now the average parishioner cannot name a single scholar or even a prominent preacher, apart from the right-wing religionists who appear on television. Even the word *Christian* currently denotes a nuanced perspective one would only occasionally find in any of the seminaries or great universities established by the traditional churches for the training of their clergy and the interpenetrating of the theological and the secular disciplines. Both politically and theologically, the liberal institutions, together with their historic and ideological derivatives, are out of style. "Christian," in the popular mind, now means "evangelical."

The Secular Assault

Consider first the secular assault on the old-line Protestant and, to an equal extent, Roman Catholic versions of the Christian faith. Yet it is not so much an assault as it is the assumption that classical Christian thought is passé, dated, and irrelevant. Perhaps not since the era of the French skeptics has religion been more widely viewed as an archaic amusement engaged in by the unenlightened. Notwithstanding popular surveys, which seem to demonstrate that most Americans still claim some belief in God and admit to engaging in some sort of prayer and worship, religion is increasingly a peripheral matter.

In the wake of the Enlightenment, as Western civilization began to discover the marvelous complexities of science, a religion that refused to come to terms with what we were finding out about the world and about ourselves was laughed off the stage of history, at least among the intellectually elite. The excoriation of Galileo, who, following Copernicus, insisted that the world was certainly neither flat nor the universe geocentric, branded those who held out against him—the religious establishment—as hopelessly outdated. Among the enlightened, one of the most enjoyable sports of the time was to poke fun at the silly religious people and their silly religious notions that continued to mildew under stultified—if still powerful—ecclesial tents. Voltaire's *Candide* remains a classic. Anyone with any sense of history, let alone the eyes to look around Europe, knew that this most certainly was not the best of all possible worlds.

The traditional Christian analysis could not stand. If the masses were still steeped in a superstition that to a large extent determined the scope and content of their daily lives, among increasing numbers of intellectuals such dated notions, and the institutions that supported them, were on the way out. It was just a matter of time. New golden models of how the universe functioned—in both its microcosmic and macrocosmic manifestations—continued to drive the cheapened currency of "Christian" cosmology from the intellectual marketplace. At one end of the spectrum, the telescope eventually took the lid off the firmament; at the other end of the spectrum, the microscope obliterated simplistic notions of everything else.

To be sure, a series of vigorous counterattacks was made. William Blake realized that the world of Sir Isaac Newton was itself limited and one-dimensional—"a single vision and Newton's sleep," he called the notions that had been set loose in the then-emerging modern world. Blake reasoned that a culture in which everything that could not be quantified and scientifically analyzed was discounted, produced little more than a dull, flat world without value, mystery, or hope. Counterattacks by the Christian humanists, centered in the great universities still largely under ecclesial control, attempted to reconcile the burgeoning fields of secular knowledge with spiritual truths and values. It was in these counterattacks—mystical and academic—that the roots of faith were preserved, even as their flowers gave off a less-than-acceptable aroma.

While holding onto certain core values, many thoughtful Christians learned to celebrate the new world as here to stay. Newton was not to be driven away by a louder recitation of the hocus-pocus that had become the staple diet in much of the popular religious environment. Both within the churches of the Reformation and within the Roman church from which they sprang, there was a concerted effort to take seriously the amazing discoveries of the Enlightenment and its cultural and intellectual heirs.

If anything thwarted this effort to see how God was bringing to birth a new world, there was within the church the rising tide of reaction. Fundamentalism was not born in the twentieth century. It has been continually cycled and recycled throughout Christian history. We will presently have a closer look at this phenomenon.

The nineteenth century brought a fresh secular challenge to the Christian experience and tradition. The great trinity of intellectual and cultural giants—Freud, Marx, and Darwin—irrevocably established the notion that a new world was not going to dissolve in a puff of smoke or dissipate on the diffused incense of the prayers of the faithful. Clearly what had been the philosophic and intellectual underpinnings of the Christian faith could never be the same. Theology could not go home again.

Part of the problem lay in the realization that not only had science begun to dominate the academic world, but also that the worldview—the philosophic structure that produced much of classical Christian theology—was no longer held. Not only was the three-tiered geocentric universe gone forever, but so was the Platonic world of ideas and forms that were substantial in the development of the historic creeds of the church. Few thinkers still divided the world into substance and accidence. Bread and wine, for instance, which was still physical bread and wine after it was properly consecrated, could not *really* have become body and blood. Nor did it make immediate sense anymore to think of God as one substance and three persons. Without the older philosophic structures, a religious system built on them found itself in serious intellectual difficulty. As long as the thoughtful (and those not so thoughtful) had both a compatible natural world and the classical philosophy that accompanied it, the creeds, the sacraments, and traditional ways to articulate the faith made sense. With the severing of these roots, the secular challenge to religion became even more severe.

Scholars began to apply these new scientific and philosophic insights to religious artifacts and sources. Not only was the Bible translated into the vernacular, but also many who took it seriously began to look again at some ancient questions left unaddressed for centuries: Who wrote, collected, edited, and translated the Bible? Did it produce the church, or did the church produce it? In what sense is it the word or words of God? Are all materials of equal importance? To what extent was the Bible conditioned by the context of those who wrote it? What was the relationship between history and story? How does its prescientific production affect what it has to say? Do readers, in whatever age, come to it out of their own context, and how does that determine what they find in the text? Literary criticism, higher and lower, provided another secular set of issues that called into question traditional understandings of theology and of the Christian life. (For a fuller treatment of these issues, see my *Building a Biblical Faith*, Chalice Press, 1995.)

It becomes clear that secularism did not suddenly emerge in the last quarter of the twentieth century, nor is it likely to disappear with the dawning of a new millennium. Traditional religionists may rail against it, foam and fume, or call it the devil's doing; but a secularized world will provide the context by which increasing numbers of Westerners will understand themselves and their universe.

While many of the religious artifacts remain, Western culture is already dominated by a secular mentality. If the authority of the church, geographically understood, is dead, so is the parallel ideological reality. The driving force that now shapes the Western world is no longer Christendom.

The demise of the local English parish is a case in point. In most places its worship services are almost empty. As religious institutions shrink, a remnant seems to hang on. This remnant usually is composed of folks who may have given up on religion but can't break the habit of going to church, as well as those who find meaning, power, and security in the historic articulation of faith and the art of the liturgy. However, in England the overt forces that determine daily life are more Freudian, Marxist, and Darwinian than they are Pauline, Wesleyan, or Lutheran—let alone the content of the good rector's Sunday discourse.

A few years back I spent a term at Cambridge University. While folks still turned out in large numbers at the marvelously crafted sung services at Kings College Chapel, there were occasionally more paid singers in the choir than folks in the pews in the community's large old Anglican parishes. The exceptions were found in spirited evangelical parishes and newly formed fundamentalist free churches. Mainline free churches, including the Methodist and the United Reformed Church—a merger of Congregational and Presbyterian bodies—were kept open by the dedication of a few older people who had given in neither to the right-wing religious expression nor to the left-wing secular expression.

The United States is not far behind these English relatives. While the symbols still remain, the dominant ethos of North America is predominantly secular. More than enough has already been written about the malaise of North American mainline religion. Those churches that formed the backbone of the religious experience have all suffered both in terms of influence and numbers. My own denomination, the Christian Church (Disciples of Christ), has seen a loss of members every year for almost three decades, and nobody, except the most oblivious optimist, looks for a reversal or even a slowing of that precipitous fall. We once boasted of having 2.5 million members, a figure probably substantially inflated by the dint of clerical pride and poor record keeping. We now claim only seven hundred thousand, a figure that is probably equally inflated.

This and most other mainline churches show all the signs of an approaching institutional demise. If institutions are born, grow, level out, decline, and die, the now sideline churches seem to be somewhere on the downside of the hill. A few of these members have drifted into fundamentalist congregations, but most of those who left have drifted out the back door into secularism. At the same time the "liberals," who formerly occupied the pews, have become committed to limiting the number of children produced by their families. The drive for zero population growth has been realized, and now these same people ask each other, "Why are there so few children in our Sunday schools?" It has been well documented that the demise of the mainline churches is partly a product of demographics.

Ecumenism, a household god among most mainliners, has also been bitten by the secular bug. A generation back there was a call by leading churchmen—there were few women in positions of religious eminence at that time—to bring into organic union the leading mainline denominations. An Episcopal bishop, James Pike, and the head of the largest Presbyterian body, Eugene Carson Blake, wondered aloud whether the time might be ripe for one great American church that would be Protestant, Catholic, and Evangelical, thus pulling together streams long separated. From Episcopalians to Congregationalists—both historic black and historic white communions—came an enthusiastic response. However, about that time the tide of popularity and power turned, as did our priorities and the way we invested energy and funds. The proposal has yet to be enacted, even though the "Consultation on Church Union" continues to explore ways by which these weakened groups can form partnerships or enter into "covenant communion"—whatever that means. While the word "Union" still exists in the title, nobody is talking merger. Every constituent body is busy trying to survive, and the energy for serious ecumenism is unavailable. Dedicated ecumenists, of which every denomination has a sturdy handful, still speak out, but fewer and fewer listen. Even if the plan of union proposed in the mid-nineties were to be enacted, chances are that ten years down the road most members of most congregations would be unable to tell the difference.

If anyone thinks that there might be wisdom in finding a common purpose among these bruised and battered bodies, the experience of almost every community where congregations of these denominations sit cheek to jowl—all three-quarters empty—should be instructive. In the city where I last served, a dozen weakened congregations are located within a six-block area, each one having a difficult time paying its heat bill, let alone its pastoral leadership. While these churches have joined with others in the community to provide significant social services—a food kitchen, food bank, a women's abuse shelter, housing for seniors, a home for pregnant unwed women, and more—the suggestion that their future lies in combining what strength they have left is greeted with resounding silence. One denomination with three diminished worshiping communities in the same part of town tried to form a common parish, but even that was beyond where their constituents were willing to go. It is as if mainline congregations are more willing to sit quietly and die slowly than to combine strength. Many formerly robust mainline churches are now small enough to work more like primary social groups, whose members cling to their long-established friendships and worship their decaying buildings.

What is true of congregations is true of their various denominational bodies. The precise reasons for this ecumenical lethargy are beyond the scope of this book, but the phenomenon is obvious. Within the last decade, three of the strongest constituent bodies in the Consultation on Church Union decided to relocate their national offices. Did they seek each other? Heavens no! One moved to Cleveland, one moved to Louisville, and one decided to relocate within Indianapolis—all at enormous expense.

What is true of congregations and denominations is paralleled by the larger ecumenical bodies, long a locus of religious power in the United States. Few municipal and fewer state Councils of Churches remain, and the once potent National Council of Churches lurches from one institutional crisis to another. We will return to this ecumenical issue in Chapter Eleven.

The scientific and philosophic earthquake that began shaking the church during the Enlightenment continues. How has the church reacted? In two quite different ways, resulting in two distinct movements that persist today. While much of the church accepted and celebrated the insights of the new order of things, a sturdy resistance developed on the backside of faith. If on one hand there came about the celebrated rise of biblical criticism, on the other hand the assertion that the Bible was the inerrant, wholly inspired word of God—indeed the very words of God—became an article of faith, indeed one of the five fundamentals. From these divergent perspectives sprang the major divisions within the contemporary Christian community. While it was only a minor blip on the historic screen, perhaps nothing dramatized the division more clearly than the famous Scopes trial of 1925.

The Evangelical Assault

If, on the one hand, mainline churches are being systematically driven to the sidelines by a virulent secularism, they are being squeezed on the other hand by a yeasty form of evangelicalism. I include classical fundamentalists and the more recently emerging charismatic bodies in this delineation. While not cut from the same cloth, these variegated faith communities are increasingly seeking ways to communicate with one another and to seek a common social, if not theological, agenda. In these circles, to be ecumenical means for Baptists and Assemblies of God to admit that the other is Christian and to seek an end to mutual recriminations and name-calling. The rest of the church is simply written off as both heretical and irrelevant.

For a decade Martin Marty has been involved in the *Fundamentalist Project*, which has taken an exhaustive look at the phenomenon. Since this evangelical tidal wave is still building, only the initial chapters have thus far been written. Just how powerful the movement has become is more evidenced by its political power than by its theological presuppositions. The congressional election of 1994 pointed up how deeply fundamentalism has become woven into the texture of the American fabric. The issue is now larger than a few mega-churches on the edge of town, or a handful of televangelists hawking religious snake oil. Nor is it simply a matter of charismatics luring large groups of people out of the mainline churches. While a few who have discovered the excitement of evangelicalism have come from the ranks of the religiously disillusioned, many more have come from the ranks of the unchurched for whom classical Protestantism met no apparent need. The loss among the mainliners has been to secularism and inner decay, not primarily to fundamentalism.

As long as conservative religion and conservative politics are juxtaposed, pulling in opposite directions, there is room in the center for rational faith. But when these two opposing forces have historically found some common ground, a new set of cultural dynamics often emerged. When the sun and the moon pull the seas in opposite directions there are normal tides. When these two bodies are in line, the tides are extraordinary. And that is the new factor that came into play beginning about 1990. The anomaly is that while the Western world is now solidly secular, at the same time there is a resurgence of conservative religion that is finding common cause with the dominant political mentality.

One would not have to dig very far into history to see what happens when a repressive political system gets tied up with an equally repressive religious institution. A long list of dark moments could be compiled in which church and state made common cause against minorities, those of other religions, the pariahs, foreigners, infidels, and other groups out of favor. Consider the Inquisition; the scandalous periodic pogroms against the Jews and, in the case of the Crusades, the Moslems; the German Christian movement of the 1920s and '30s. Consider further the history of Latin America, beginning with Columbus and continuing through the first two thirds of the twentieth century. In North America, when conservative religion and a conservative political system made common cause, the results were the Salem witch trials in the North and the support of slavery and segregation in the South. The situation is exacerbated in nondemocratic lands. Let a rigid political system align itself with a rigid religious system, and there is going to be trouble for everyone else in the neighborhood.

In his insightful book about the relationship between Jews and Arabs, David Shipler quotes a prominent Israeli rabbi, David Hartman. "Religion...is fundamentally reactionary, not pluralistic....You can use God to expel the Arabs from every inch of this territory, and you can use God and the Bible and Jewish tradition to say that there shouldn't be any Christians in this country and there shouldn't be any deviation from pure monotheism." Shipler goes on to comment that when the moderate ground is eaten away religion becomes a force for evil. "It coats warfare and terrorism and hatred with a varnished righteousness." Great wrongs are often done in the name of religious purity. "The believer certainty carries a curse against whoever stands outside." Shipler's point is that in Israel, the issue is exacerbated by political figures on both sides who, although not religious themselves, use the fundamentalist's religious zeal as an excuse to perpetuate long-standing hostilities (David K. Shipler, *Arab and Jew*, Penguin Books, 1986).

What is true in the troubled land Shipler describes has been true throughout history whenever conservative religion and conservative politics make common cause. No other form of tyranny has been as persistent and as fraught with inhumanity than this unholy and anti-human combination.

While in certain sections of the United States there has long been a comfortable relationship between right-wing politics and right-wing religion, these forces have now joined to form the dominant social ethos, and therein lies the danger. The evangelical wave developed a rhythmic continuity with a fresh conservative populism now at the center of the political landscape. For most of our modern history, at least since the dawning of the New Deal of the 1930s, right-wing politics existed on the edge of the American agenda—and so did right-wing religion. Carl McIntire was little more than a raucous voice, a yapping hound snapping at the heels of the nation's liberal agenda and the mainline churches that supported it. Pat Robertson is not so easily defined. For better or worse, the United States may now be standing at the doorway of a powerful conservative phase of a historic cycle. We are just now beginning to measure the dramatic effects of this development.

Consider how advocates of this conservative agenda articulate the relationship between church and state. For a number of years a hot debate has raged over the intention of the nation's founders regarding the relationship between our national identity and the Christian faith. Evangelicals cite scores of statements suggesting that we were, from the outset, a Christian nation. In his book *The Myth of Separation—To Pray or Not to Pray*, David Barton asserts that all the founding fathers, with the possible exception of Benjamin Franklin, were evangelicals. The first amendment to the Constitution, he holds, and the subsequent "wall of separation" were promulgated to keep one European-based denomination from dominating other Christian bodies. The assertion is then made that more recent decisions by the Supreme Court maul the Constitution and the original intent of the founders. Christianity, so say these conservative religionists—indeed a specific reading of the faith—is the sure rock on which the United States is founded.

At the edge of this "Christian America" movement, the "Reconstructionists" want to establish a theocracy, ruled by conservative Christians and inhospitable to all others. According to Barton, only the righteous have the right to hold office. America is seen as the locus of God's kingdom and the citadel of divine power until Jesus returns. Indeed, God chose the United States as the new Israel. It is here that the returned Christ will set up the new order for a thousand years—but only if the United States returns to the theocratic government and ethos the founders of the nation envisaged. While many early leaders may have uttered pious sentiments, they were also clear that there would be no theocracy on these shores. The word "God" never appears in the Constitution, and religion—prior to the First Amendment—is alluded to only once, and that to disavow any religious test for office. At best the nation's founders were agnostics, who still made religious allusions in their public rhetoric. When it came to codification and law writing, their position is clear. Church and state were to exist side by side, respectful of each other, but separated by a sturdy wall.

Other contemporary evangelicals hold to a much more open agenda. While insisting that the intention of the founders was to establish a Christian nation, they admit that the United States is now pluralistic, and ask only that "Christians" find a place at the table.

The Secular Domination of Western Culture

Despite what may be a "Christian" rear-guard action, increasingly the thrust of secularism grows more powerful. While evangelicals flail—sometimes with spasmodic thrusts of political power—they are no match for the enormous power of our increasingly irreligious culture. For better or for worse, secularism is the dominant note in the American melody. The moral tone, language, institutional power, and control of the time and energy of every age group in the nation are clearly in nonreligious hands. We are members of a secular society. While the evangelical community has vigorously responded to this secularization, the mainline churches remain clueless.

In the 1993 book by Yale law professor Stephen L. Carter, *The Culture of Disbelief*, there is an intriguing analysis of this emergence of a nonreligious ethos in the United States. While Carter wants to challenge the secular power brokers in the name of traditional religious belief, I find the point he really makes is that for now the battle is lost. While it is easy to decry sexual libertinism, greed, materialism, violence, and all the rest, it is less easy to develop, let alone put in place, a systemic corrective. It may be, as we shall later spell out in greater detail, a matter of large historic tides or cycles. The question may not be "How do we reverse the trend?" but "How do we survive until the cycle moves on and the tides flood in?"

Carter asks: What does it mean to restore "religion to the place of honor that it deserves in the pantheon of American cultural institutions?" (p. 68). The evangelical response notwithstanding, I doubt that there is any simple programmatic agenda the mainline church can develop, given the present cultural environment, that will answer Carter's question. This book is not, however, a call to inaction, but the affirmation that mainline churches must seek to cast a different agenda, even as they struggle to maintain institutional strength sufficient to take the initiative again when this conservative phase of the cycle gives way to a brighter day. There are, in the meantime, a whole series of things religious "liberals" can and must do. Unless we get about these tasks we will not survive the ebb tide, but will dry out and fossilize on the arid beaches of culture, and will have nothing left to offer when history moves beyond this current secular-fundamentalist episode. While by keeping the pressure on we may nudge the larger historic movement, we cannot develop ten easy ways to turn back the power of secularism. We will not manufacture a program or a mind-set that will either reestablish the good old days or bring about a new world. The reign of God comes by God's action. While heralding God's coming reign, we are called to provide demonstration projects as to what it will look like. But we do not build the

Kingdom! What we do is learn how to sing the Lord's song even in a strange land.

The notes and rhythms of this music will be spelled out later in the book.

The Mainline Church in an Ebbing Tide

The mainline church has been caught in an ebbing tide. The conservative wave is heady, but it will not persist indefinitely. Those committed to turning back history's clocks never do very well for very long. The modern world will not be silenced by those shouting Bible verses. Fundamentalism may persist for a few decades, at most. It will pass. It always has. But for now what was once mainline religion is being squeezed dry between secularism and evangelicalism. The remainder of this book seeks to address how we maintain our integrity and how we husband enough institutional strength against the day the tide turns and the conservative cycle and its agenda—both politically and religiously—fades.

When Judah went into its seventy years of Babylonian captivity, the people refused to sing the Lord's songs in public places. But sing them they did, to their children, and the children remembered. When the tide turned and Cyrus came to the throne, these children went home strong enough to rebuild Jerusalem and its temple. In this in-between-the-tides era, how can an authentic Christian faith maintain enough strength and integrity to teach its children the Lord's songs? This book seek to provide some clues leading to an answer to that question.

In the next chapter we will look at some tempting directions and their alluring siren voices.

Questions for Reflection and Discussion

1. Think about the religious leaders whose work and thought are important in your life and in the life of your congregation. What are their names? What is the extent of their influence? How did they become well known to you and the members of your church? What is it they believe? Where do they currently serve or teach?

2. Given the power and influence of science and technology, and the secular hegemony which is well in place in our culture, what roles do religion and religious thought play in our society? Do you draw your opinions about such things as war, race, poverty, and the protection of the environment from secular or sacred sources? When planning your weekly schedules and commitments, what influence does secularism have, and to what extent are decisions made on spiritual, religious, or theological grounds? Or is the matter even given much thought?

3. There was an era when the Bible seemed to draw the boundaries of its own authority. Sometime back we began to apply the tools of literary science to it. Has the Bible lost its influence, its aura, and its mystery? If so, what has replaced it? Do you sometimes wonder if the names Freud, Marx, and Darwin have more to do with daily life than Moses, Paul, or even Jesus?

4. Would you say that the mainline churches in your community are doing well? What is their influence beyond the families that make them up? When the local press talks about "Christians," do they mean you, or have the mainline churches been replaced by fundamentalists and charismatics? List the new congregations that have been planted in your community in recent years. What are they like? To what denominations do they belong? What is their influence?

5. Do you sense any change in the way religion is affecting public policy? Are issues such as prayer in the public schools, abortion, and programs for the poor and marginalized influenced by the religious community? If so, what part of it and how does your religion affect these and similar cultural issues?

6. Do you consider the United States to be a Christian nation? How does religion exercise influence in the public square? Is its effect increasing or decreasing?

2 | How Shall the Mainline Church Respond?

Threatened institutions have at their command a variety of possible responses. The threat may be perceived as external or internal, an interruption of expected progress or a death threat, a temporary setback or what appears to be long-range trouble. How the response is framed will determine most future possibilities. Some institutions, and some persons, for that matter, are immobilized when confronted with a serious challenge, while others move quickly to take action. In this chapter we will examine and evaluate a number of potential responses currently before the formerly powerful mainline churches and their denominations. Consider the following possibilities, all of which are in our active vocabulary. The question before us is, How shall we expend our energies and define our vision and role in the short term—or until the tide turns?

We can redig the old wells and attempt to recapture our former glory.

We can learn from and mimic those who have become the power brokers and the powerful.

We can reject the power brokers and the powerful, and spend our energies fighting them off.

We can admit that we had our day, grow old, and die gracefully.

We can redefine our identity and our mission and seek to embody a new image, free from the restraints of the old image.

We can use what is appropriate from all of the above and wait for the right moment to seize the initiative.

St. Paul's Faces the Future

As we review the different possible approaches presented in this chapter, we will do so from the perspective of a fictional, but all too typical, mainline congregation.

St. Paul's Church, Central City, USA, is about to celebrate its fiftieth anniversary. Its planting was carefully thought through by the old First Church downtown—a congregation that closed five years ago. The denomination, as well as the Comity Commission of the local Council of Churches, also had a hand. St. Paul's began its life with the gift of five acres of land in a burgeoning new residential area at what was then the edge of the city. The judicatory provided the land through a "Builders Club," which solicited twenty dollars each from hundreds of members of other churches. It received its first fifty members from the mother congregation. After three years of worshiping in a rented grade school auditorium, ground was broken for the first unit: a multipurpose educational building with a central hall suitable for both dinners and worship.

St. Paul's growth in its first decade was exponential. Ten years after it had occupied the original unit, a sanctuary seating 450 worshipers was constructed; within two years the church needed to employ a second pastor and decided to institute a second Sunday morning service. At its zenith St. Paul's boasted twelve hundred members and an average worship attendance of 650. The weekly church school attendance was even larger than the worshiping congregation. Classes were filled with enthusiastic young families, who saw the church as the center of their religious, social, and civic lives. The congregation gave substantial amounts of money to denominational mission and administrative enterprises. St. Paul's could be counted on to take the leadership in causes for the common good, including civil rights and service to the poor and marginalized.

Early in the '70s the numerical indices began to level out. The senior pastor, who had occupied the pulpit for fifteen years, was called to one of the five largest congregations in the denomination. Each of the three pastors who followed lasted less than two years. Careful observers noted that the community had also stabilized. While not inner-city, St. Paul's was no longer at the edge of town. The once new homes were now several decades old. They had been built too quickly and too cheaply and now looked tired. So did St. Paul's.

Since the leveling-out period, each annual report has seen a diminishing of resources, new members, and the size of the worshiping congregation. Some years the decline was negligible, but in the last decade the slide has been precipitous. Worship attendance on a good day is now one hundred, and church school attendance is fewer than that. The children's sermon presently garners three or four youngsters, and there is no active youth group. The average age of the active members is over sixty. The building is in need of major repairs, for which there are no funds.

What is true of St. Paul's is true of many other mainline congregations in its city. There are now in this community three megachurches, one Baptist, one Assembly of God, and the third an independent congregation built around its charismatic founding pastor. A handful of St. Paul's members have found a home in one of these three other bodies, but nobody really knows what has happened to most of those no longer seen around the church. They seem to have disappeared. The truth is that many have died or are now too infirm to make it to worship. A number have moved away, including youth who went away to college and found jobs elsewhere. The former stalwarts have not been replaced. Still another large group has simply melted into the secular culture. While they still consider themselves Christians, their lives, habits, attitudes, and commitments are no longer church related. Sunday is their only day to do the wash or to engage in family outings. Since both members of most married couples are employed during the week, they are not ready to be scheduled on Sundays. The affluent have cabins on a nearby lake, and the less affluent find their children involved in sports activities and a score of other functions that keep them from church school. These families have been taken over not by some other religious commitment but by secularism.

It has become obvious to the leaders at St. Paul's that theirs is a dying church. A highly visible task force is appointed to determine how the congregation might respond to what is perceived to be an impending crisis. Each of the following scenarios is actively considered by the task force.

"We Can Redig the Old Wells"

Every institution that has a golden era in its memory celebrates its past but must insist psychologically that the best days are yet to come. At least that is what the leaders keep telling everybody. New pastors begin their ministries by saying, "I was not sent here to bury St. Paul's!" To ignore the values in the history of any institution is to cut off its life's blood. There are persons, points of view, dynamics, and a vision that live in the active memories of every vital church body. Knowing and retelling these stories are always critical to the future of a troubled congregation. If a combination of energies, points of view, dynamics, and persons made it what it once was, perhaps the secret lies in recasting the present situation by using the old tools. In this perspective, as in each of the others we shall outline in this chapter, there is more than a thread of truth. But here there is also a thick cable of nostalgia and wishful thinking. If history were static we could go back to the founders and discover the clues to success. But history is dynamic, always on the move and always changing, and what worked in one age may not be appropriate for another.

More than one denomination has had as its vision the restoration of "the ancient order of things." Underlying this assumption is the notion that the church following Pentecost sprang perfect and pure from the intention of God and the mind and work of the apostles. The apostolic church is seen therefore as a model of what the church in every time and in every place ought to be. One simply needs to replicate that pattern. Everything since the apostolic period that differs from the original form is in error to the extent of the difference. Obviously this notion is both theoretically and practically useless. There was no single form or formula in the apostolic period. The church in one place did not look like, act like, or believe like the church in another place. Corinth and Jerusalem were very different. But so were Corinth and Ephesis. The Jerusalem conference, recorded in Acts 15, not only admitted but codified some of these differences.

The New Testament, however, remains our most reliable source for the history of this first period. If these records are in any sense normative or offer a pattern for the life of the church today, what is to be made of the fact that much of the New Testament was not even written, let alone collected, translated, or received canonical status, for centuries? What is more, a simple analysis of the Gospels demonstrates how even they grew out of different and quite unreconcilable perspectives. And what is one to make of the twenty intervening centuries? Has the Holy Spirit been absent for two millennia? Restorationists universally suffer from what might be called a severe case of cultivated historic discontinuity.

The problem is compounded in an institution, in this case a congregation, that feels its power waning. While it might be possible to recapture some of the spirit and energy of a former golden age (whether you have in mind the first century or the 1940s), often the effort is futile.

The first possibility presented to the task force at St. Paul's was to replicate the conditions that once made the congregation a powerhouse. This possibility took two forms. First, they considered going back to the beginning of their history and doing again what once had been done. That is, they might find five acres on the edge of town and start over. At present St. Paul's has more members than did the chartered congregation. It is assumed that the present building could be sold to some other group, probably evangelicals or African Americans who have recently invaded the neighborhood. However, discreet inquiries about the sale of the building proved discouraging. The CEO of the hospital next door, when asked about the possibilities that the medical community might want the building, responded, "What's a used church worth?" In time the building might be marketed to another congregation, but that could take years, which would leave St. Paul's without resources to purchase land.

The assumption that none of their members lived in the neighborhood anymore was shattered when they charted where the active congregants actually resided. To the surprise of the task force, there were more pins within a mile of the present location than in any other place on the map.

St. Paul's also received less-than-enthusiastic reports about congregations their denomination had recently planted in suburban communities. These churches were not achieving the same growth St. Paul's had at its inception. Many had constructed first units and never grew out of them. Among the handful of churches the judicatory was forced to close each year, several were more recently organized groups that were unable to take root and could not survive economically. It became obvious that this was not the day of the mainline church. In the denomination there were substantial, thriving, newly minted congregations; but these tended to be among Hispanic or African-American populations, not white middle-class groups. While the idea struck a positive cord, churches of this and other mainline denominations simply could not replicate the successful models of half a century ago.

While it is true that numbers of mainline congregations have survived and even flourished by relocating, that is not the rule. People who inhabit new communities are not breathlessly waiting for the appearance of a liberal congregation. The day is gone—at least for now—when these denominations can put up a building with the assurance that it will soon be filled. What is more, the escalation of land and building costs, and the limitation of resources in the judicatories, make this endeavor increasingly difficult.

St. Paul's task force discovered that relocating was not the only way to redig the old wells. The group set about taking a serious look at their own history. What was the church doing that generated the massive support it had once enjoyed? Most of the materials focused around Rev. Williams. "He packed them in!" said one of the old timers on the task force. "We need to find somebody just like him," added another member.

"We have neglected our young people. If we had the best youth director we could find, our future would be secure."

Someone discovered that the church formerly held week-long preaching services. Other groups might have called these extended meetings "revivals," but St. Paul's had always been too sophisticated to use that term. Nevertheless, the annual, carefully orchestrated "festival of preaching" had turned out newcomers in substantial numbers, many of whom joined the church. There were the large, organized adult church school classes, and hundreds of women who met during the day in a score of circles. All-church dinners were held every Friday night, and visiting missionaries kept the wider interests of the congregation in full view. The congregation was also deeply involved with other similar churches in a broad range of ecumenical activities.

The suggestion was put forward that every effort be made to do again what had been done in the golden age. While the project looked good on paper, it finally dawned on the task force that it was impossible to turn back the clock. This was a different age, and nobody quite knew how to do the old things anymore. Redigging the wells would not solve St. Paul's problem.

"If They Can Do It, Why Can't We?"

The task force turned to a second option. One of the solid businesswomen suggested that common sense dictated the congregation look around, see who was thriving, and learn from them. If your program to lose weight—or in this case to gain weight—works, and mine doesn't, I must have something to learn from you. Weak institutions looking over their shoulders at strong institutions might grow from mimicking their neighbors. Again, there is a certain amount of truth here. Persons and institutions that assume they have all the answers wall themselves in when they arrogantly assert they have nothing to learn from anybody else.

Members of St. Paul's task force spent several weeks visiting the three thriving congregations in the community, interviewing their pastors, and talking informally with members they knew in their neighborhoods and workplaces. It quickly became clear that St. Paul's was out of step. There were identifiable marks of successful congregations, just as there were marks of dying ones.

It was discovered that all three of the rapidly growing churches were in harmony with the prevailing political ethos of the city. That is, they were all conservative in a conservative political environment. If the mainline congregations were being squeezed by a combination of conservative religion and conservative politics, the successful churches had no such problem. Not only were the political positions of the congregations clear, but their members also formed the backbone of the dominant conservative mind-set of the community. These three congregations, and smaller ones with similar postures, set the religious agenda of the city. When anyone wondered what the "Christian" position was on a variety of issues, these churches and their members made it clear. No "it might be this and it might be that." There weren't any gray areas. It was simple enough for everybody to grasp:

- Abortion is murder.
- Gays and lesbians stand condemned.
- Mom, Dad, and the children constitute the only valid family constellation.
- Capital punishment has divine approval.
- Any effort to control the availability of handguns is un-American, and therefore unchristian.
- Society needs more prisons and longer sentences.
- The poor are lazy and immoral, and therefore welfare programs should be cut to reduce taxes on the middle class.
- Military budgets should be increased, but social programs should be reduced because they tend to be "pork."
- Christian observances should be officially reinstated in tax-supported schools.
- America's borders should be sealed, and illegal aliens excluded from medical and educational benefits.

At the same time, these evangelicals took serious objection to what they saw going on in the larger society. They viewed with alarm what they felt to be the disintegration of morality, the loss of solid family structures, the widespread disrespect for authority, the failure of public education to maintain order—let alone decency—and the sexualization of popular culture. Without moral absolutes, the world seemed to be crumbling around them. They, too, were interested in redigging the old wells—going back and restoring a golden age that was orderly, less fixated on sex, and more under the control of responsible men—meaning males. The more they and conservative politicians listened to each other, the more in agreement they were, thus forming, if not a solid majority, at least the most vocal and clearly defined growing minority.

St. Paul's, on the other hand, had long taken quite a different social posture, and it was obvious that what it had traditionally held about the relationship between the Christian faith and the rest of the world was out of style—in fact, clearly negative. A member of the task force suggested that if St. Paul's was to survive, it had to be more like the three congregations that were thriving. And yet, as they looked carefully at the political agendas that they found in these bodies, they concluded that it was far from the gracious gospel of Christ, as they had always understood it. To adopt these agendas would be to trade faithfulness for success, and the task force was not prepared to move in that direction.

Not only did these three booming congregations differ from St. Paul's in terms of their social policies, but these churches also took the Bible as the inerrant, perfect, inspired word of God. GOD SAID IT. I BELIEVE IT. THAT SETTLES IT! The differences between black and white, good and evil, right and wrong were clear. The Bible told the truth, and the pastor's job was to take the Bible and tell folks what it said, without question or reservation. New people who came to these congregations were never left in doubt as to the meaning of faith or exactly what faith required.

The programs of these winners differed markedly from the program at St. Paul's.

It began with worship. Each of the three had transformed their chancels into sound stages, with batteries of microphones, banks of loudspeakers, and space for a collection of modern amplified instruments, sets of drums, and several electronic keyboards. Strangely enough, the pulpits—behind which the pastors rarely stood—were all Plexiglas. Worship was, in a word, exciting! People were turned on. Applause followed every event on the program. Everybody prayed out loud all at once.

What is more, bad weather, good weather, the youth basketball league, or the long work week didn't seem to keep the members away. They flocked in. The reason was clear to anyone who looked. As the pastor of the largest of the three put it, "When people come here they expect to cut loose and have a good time—and they do."

Each congregation had its own grade school to which the faithful were pressured to send their children. Bible study was expected, not only on Sunday morning but in groups throughout the week. These parishioners believed that the world out there was evil, and so "Christians" were expected to spend more and more of their lives within the church and among other church members. Whatever these three congregations were doing—it worked! Perhaps St. Paul's best hope was to mimic the evangelicals. Or was it?

"Fight Them Every Step of the Way!"

The third option presented to St. Paul's task force was to declare war on the forces of secularism as well as on the forces of conservative religion. It would be simultaneously a defensive and an offensive effort. The mainline churches, so went this line of reasoning, are essentially correct, both in their political and in their religious analysis. Why should they give over to despair or stand quietly while they are beaten around the head and shoulders by negative, aggressive, and clearly wrongheaded groups with wrongheaded political ideologies?

The secular society was not to be worshiped but to be taken on. Science is not our shepherd, and the world without God is not a world worth living in. Members of the church must be called back from secularism. Perhaps St. Paul's had been too soft and too permissive for too long. Perhaps it had lost its moral imperative over the years by allowing folks to get away with sloppy spiritual habits, such as sitting quietly while the culture commandeered Sunday for whatever it wanted. Perhaps St. Paul's needed to develop a discipline to which its members would be called. If the secular juggernaut could not be stopped, perhaps the congregation could etch out a territory and guard it from any further encroachment. Maybe secularism could even be driven back.

If fighting off the secularity of culture is to war against the tides with a feather, the more immediate problem appeared to be to maintain a clearing in the jungle of religious conservatism. To allow the nonreligious world to assume that the public policy articulated by right-wing religion is in fact the Christian gospel is to be faithless. The religious agenda outlined on page 22 seemed to the task force to be far removed from the teachings of Jesus. St. Paul's had long viewed the Scriptures as the foundation and root of Christian ethics—personal and social. But they had seen in the biblical tradition a far different understanding of the social order than did the evangelicals, particularly as it applied to a number of contemporary issues.

- Neither Jesus, nor anyone else in Christian scriptures, ever discussed abortion. The only reference anywhere in the Hebrew scriptures is a prescription for producing a miscarriage to satisfy a jealous husband (Numbers 5:11–31).

How Shall the Mainline Church Respond? 25

- Jesus never mentioned homosexuality, let alone condemned it, although he certainly must have known numbers of men and women with that lifestyle.
- Jesus had little to say about typical families. He insisted that all those who did God's will were members of his family (Matthew 12:46–50). The only sword he came to bring would divide families (Matthew 10:34–39).
- Jesus never supported capital punishment, or any other form of violence, even in self-defense. He declared the old law of "an eye for an eye, and a tooth for a tooth," to be null and void (Matthew 6:38–48).
- In his first recorded sermon, Jesus declared that his mission included setting the captives free and bringing justice to the oppressed. This proclamation, made in Nazareth to the displeasure of his audience, also affirmed that God's arms were wide open to detested foreigners (Luke 4:16–30).
- Handguns? He held that those who live by the sword would die by the sword, and he prohibited his followers from taking up arms even to save his life (Matthew 26:47–52).
- Jesus took a dim view of public praying, and was particularly wary of pray-ers who held others in disdain (Luke 18:9–14).
- Jesus' encounter with a tax collector resulted in half the collections being returned to the poor (Luke 19:1–10).

The task force considered inviting the congregation to spend considerable time, effort, and funds keeping alive a social agenda that challenged the evangelicals at almost every point.

"We've Fought the Good Fight, but Our Day Is Over"

A member of the task force, who saw himself as a "realist," suggested yet another option. His argument rested on the assumption that every institution has a life cycle, and that effort spent keeping a church alive in a religious Intensive Care Unit is not only poor stewardship, but also a waste of time. "We have done what we were called to do and be. Now let's die gracefully. We'll maintain a congregation as long as there are enough people to pay the bills; but when the day comes we can't hold things together economically, we'll turn over the property and what resources we have to someone else and have an enormous going-out party."

God, it was suggested, is not limited to one way of doing things. What serves God's purposes in one generation cannot and will not serve them in a different world. St. Paul's, indeed the entire mainline church enterprise, was important for a long time. But that day is over. It is now sideline, not mainline. It will soon die. In addition, the institution is so set in its ways of thinking and doing that it would be an impossible task to recast it into something very different. Better to let it go and give our attention to whatever new thing God is ready to bring into being.

While that argument had a certain appeal, other members of the task force were convinced that the residual power of the congregation was much larger than might be otherwise assumed, and that any talk of death with dignity was premature.

"Let's Be the New Thing!"

Two of the younger members of the task force offered quite a different scenario. "Let's start over right here. No, we will not attempt to replicate what our grandparents did a half century ago. Nor will we try to restore anything. We will let the present congregation do its thing, but we will organize a new church in this building. We will begin by challenging a few of the younger, more adventurous members of the congregation, and comb the neighborhood for as many others as we can find who might be willing to make a fresh start. We'll begin a new earlier worship service, but we will not use our sanctuary. We will use the social hall downstairs. It will be a folk service, very informal, without organ, hymnals, creeds, eucharist, robes, candles, ushers, church school, circles, committees, or any of the other baggage that goes with the old way. We will find someone to play the guitar. We may write a few of our own songs. The children will sit on the floor and be allowed to be children, not silent little adults. We will spend a long time finding out what people need and want—mostly people who have never been part of a church before. We will design our services and procedures while we are on the trail."

The idea generated more positive response from other members of the task force than any scenario that had yet been considered. The more hesitant and conservative older members knew immediately that this wasn't for them, but as long as what they needed and enjoyed was not going to be disturbed, they were at least willing to listen a while longer.

A few had serious misgivings about how far a group could stray from what it had once been and still maintain any continuity with its history. How much different could this new group be and still be called St. Paul's Church? Surely there are essentials that cannot be discarded simply because they are not what people seem to want. And when history moves on will this suggested program die with the change? While the task force was not ready to reject the suggestion out of hand, neither was it ready to endorse it as the way to save St. Paul's.

One other scenario was suggested, but that will have to wait for the next chapter.

Questions for Reflection and Discussion

1. This chapter focuses on a series of possible solutions suggested by members of St. Paul's church to its world of diminishing strength and influence. Think about each of these alternatives in terms of the congregation you know best. Do you find any one of them more helpful than the others? Which? Do you sense that if your congregation is to survive it must seek new avenues of service and witness?

2. If your congregation is unlike St. Paul's, think about other congregations of your denomination in your area. Are any of them facing problems similar to those confronting St. Paul's? Would you say that your denomination and its congregations are in good shape? In the past three or four decades have they grown or shrunk, increased in strength or waned? What does the future look like if current trends persist?

3. If you were a denominational executive and were called to do an evaluation of St. Paul's, what might you suggest? Can you cite places where your line of advice has proved effective in turning around a difficult situation?

4. Did your congregation have a golden era? If so, when was it, and what was life in the church like?

5. All institutions, like all persons, have a life cycle. If you would chart your congregation's existence from its birth until its eventual death, where would you currently put it on that time-line? Is it young and dependent, mature, thriving, middle-aged, old and tired, experiencing a revival of energy, near death?

6. Are there persons in your congregation eager to go back to some golden era in church life?

7. Are there growing energetic churches in your community you might wish to emulate? If so, what makes them both attractive or authentic—and is there a difference?

8. If you could put what your church stands for on a bumper sticker, what would it say?

9. List the new programs your congregation has attempted in the past ten years. Which have worked? Which have failed? Now define how each of them flows from the faith held by your members.

3 | Staying Authentic Today While Preparing for Tomorrow

We now come to the sixth alternative answer to the question, "How can St. Paul's survive in an adverse era?" The answer we suggest will be the foundation on which the remainder of this book rests. Our thesis is not overly simplistic or triumphalistic, but neither is it without hope. It presupposes the following cultural analysis.

History has often before gone through periods adverse to authentic Christian faith. These periods tend to come about whenever conservative religion makes common cause with conservative politics. Sometimes these episodes last for a long time—centuries. Sometimes they pass more quickly. The duration rests on a number of factors mainly within the secular culture, although at times within the religious establishment. When the cycle has finally moved on, it has been important that in the interim a small, albeit disciplined, faithful church has been kept as strong as possible. The most recent example may be the witness of the underground Confessing Church in Nazi Germany.

If, in our age, secular scientism appears to be the enemy—or at least one branch of it—it can also be our friend. The modern world is too deeply entrenched to be inhibited by reactionary religious forces. Neither the Enlightenment nor the world of Freud, Marx, Darwin, Einstein, and a host of others can or will be turned back. The evangelical tide may be short-lived to the extent its flood is based on the assumption that the modern world can be discounted and we will shortly return to a prescientific social order with its inerrant Bible, rigid moral code, and quasi-theocratic forms of government. As long as a conservative political system can make use of religion, the comfortable relationship that exists between them will remain intact. When conservative religion begins to get in the way of economic progress, the secular world will move on without it.

Consider a straw in the wind that blew through the present coalition as early as the winter of 1994–95. The dominant political system had, at its root, the commitment to shrink the size, expense, and intrusive impact of government. To that end it decided that certain welfare programs had to be drastically cut or eliminated, including assistance to unmarried teenage mothers. But it became clear that jettisoning these programs would markedly increase the number of potential abortions. Conservative religionists grew very nervous. As long as conservative religion could serve the purposes of the political establishment, all was well. In fact, the symbiotic relationship between these two forces made each a welcome colleague to the other. But beyond the question of abortion, the larger issue revolved around how, and to what extent, a right-wing political economic agenda and a right-wing religious and social agenda could remain under the same tent. If, as many observed, the conservative religious fervor were to reach its zenith and could no longer promise increased numbers of votes or the extension of grass roots political organizing, its agenda would have to give way to more popular economic concerns. In the long run, Americans will vote with their pocketbooks. Given the inherent overriding power of secularism, the coalition rests on sand, and may not long survive.

In the meantime, while having little effect on that internal struggle, authentic religion must do the following: *keep its sails well trimmed, stay the course; be what it has been at its best; know when to resist the oppressive forces, both religious and political; maintain a hearty core of people who are well trained, disciplined, literate, and strong; let die what cannot be salvaged or has outlived its effectiveness and authenticity; dis-*

cover what is useful in new forms of faith, no matter from what quarter those insights come—"make friends with unrighteous mammon"— seek fresh ways of thinking and acting; and wait out the current storm. This agenda has implications for everything the congregation does, from its Sunday worship format to its concerns for social reformation. Beyond the congregation, there are implications for denominations and their judicatories, and for the larger ecumenical church in both its local and its wider manifestations.

The Conservative Agenda: Believing Our Message and Trusting Our History

Drawing on what is instructive from each of the five scenarios detailed in Chapter Two, St. Paul's Church can position itself to await the sunrise. While in Babylonian captivity, the people of God redug some old wells and passed on those traditions to their children. At the same time they borrowed much from their Babylonian captors in terms of both religion and culture, even while refusing to be Babylonians and resisting what could not be accommodated. While in Babylon an entire generation died, and with it many of the old ways brought from Jerusalem. When Cyrus came to the throne, a very different people returned to Jerusalem to rebuild the temple and reconstitute the faith. Yet theirs was a culture tied to a history that had made them a people.

If mainline religion is to emerge from this politically conservative epoch with any strength, first of all it must believe its own message and trust its own history. While we cannot and must not seek to restore some golden age, we have offered the world a way to experience, understand, and be encountered by the God of history. We are not some religious sport, springing up suddenly and dying just as suddenly. We have, in fact, a twenty-century-long, and longer, tradition. While no religious system or theological viewpoint bears eternal or infallible credentials, we have been governed by sturdy, persistent verities. At our core we know we have been encountered by and responded faithfully to a gracious God, who meets us in the processes of life and in all that is noble and redemptive. Jesus Christ, who is all of God we can see and experience in human form, has defined for us what God is like by his life, teachings, passion, and spiritual progeny. Central to our affirmation lies an encounter with the One who lives in our midst as energy, purpose, and compassion. We believe that this abiding and indefatigable God is constantly at work on our behalf.

The Bible contains our primary witness as to how God has encountered others before our own era. Along with the Bible comes the historic faith as it has been lived out over these two millennia. As the Jesuit George Tavard reminded us a generation ago, faith rests on both Holy Writ and Holy Church. Yet we know that God has always been far more inclusive than pictured in our documents, doctrines, images, or even our parochial history. Harry Emerson Fosdick once prayed to the One who "loves each one of us as if there were no one else to love, but loves all even as he loves each." We live in the blessed hope that God's will shall be done on earth and that the reign of God will overcome all human perversity. Yet we also live in the ambiguity which is hesitant to predict beyond that broad image. In the meantime, we experience an imperfect, unfinished, and sinful world.

We believe that the church is one of God's gifts to us. When it is at its best, it bears God's image and does God's work. It is not simply a social experiment. It is the way Christ is embodied in history. Church life varies with time, place, and circumstance, even as the God of history moves and changes within these boundaries. What we do affects God, just as what God is about lies at the root of all that we are and think. We do not go back to God as if God were encapsulated in any long-gone period of time. We always are on the road with God, who is ahead of us and in our midst. The Baals of the Hebrew scriptures were limited to a specific geography and people. They were static deities. The God of the Hebrews was a fellow sojourner, not limited by time and space, and not confined to the history of a particular people. Through Abraham all the nations of the earth would ultimately be blessed. Perhaps the building of Jerusalem's temple amounted to little more than the celebration of a very expansive Baal, who existed in a limited geography and was worshiped at a very elaborate high place; that is why the prophets had such difficult things to say about temple religion. As important as was the temple, for Jews the Torah was and is at the heart of faith.

Our task, as Christians and members of God's church, is to demonstrate the reality of the Reign that is to come, to be a landing party, a beachhead of the new order in the midst of the old order. We both experience and proclaim God's grace by our graciousness, works of compassion, commitment to justice and peace, care of the fragile, removers of walls that separate God's children from one another, searchers for truth, and celebraters of God's work in nature as well as in history. To forget who we are and to whom we belong, and devolve into neighborhood groups whose main task is to provide food, fun, and fellowship for people of all ages and interests, is to have nothing ultimate or even important to say. To the extent the mainline churches have failed to remain theologically rooted communities and have become competitors in the marketplace, attempting to meet everybody's social needs, we have little to offer and not much reason to live. Others in our modern affluent society do all those tasks much better than we ever can.

The first task of the mainline church in this adverse era, therefore, is to become again a center of theological inquiry, telling the story of God and God's people to its members, children, and all those with ears to hear. Local pastors must see that one of their primary tasks is to be a teacher of theology, rabbi, theologian in residence. Far down the list would be the roles of manager, marketer, program developer, recruiter, psychologist, cheerleader, and glad-hander.

The life of the congregation must gather around its storytellers, those who know the tradition and can recite it. As we shall see later, Christian education is a theological task. There is more to church schools—or in whatever format the congregation teaches its children—than learning to share toys. It is the education of these teachers, and other adults, that leavens the entire congregation. Herein lies the fundamental pastoral task.

We must believe our own message. Yet we must also winnow out the decorative and occasionally poisonous chaff from the grain of the gospel. At heart is the journey we make with the gracious God of history, who is with us and among us, known most clearly in Jesus of Nazareth. While we hold that God's grace is not limited to Christians, for us Jesus is all of God we can experience in human form.

The Receptive Agenda: Learning from Our Captors
The Gifts of Fundamentalism

While refusing to mimic either the successful fundamentalists or the dominant secularists, we are driven to affirm that they may have much to teach us. Consider what we might learn from our conservative religious antagonists. Historically, evangelical movements often served as correctives to a flaccid and irresolute traditional church. It is the sick body that is more susceptible to incursions of strange viruses. The Reformation in Europe and the revivalistic awakenings in North America called back to faith religious institutions that had lost their way. The recent renaissance of right-wing religion is in part the product of the failures of mainline religion. For instance, because we abdicated ministries of healing—except as we affirmed science—we produced the Oral Roberts and the Benny Hinns of the religious right wing. In humility we must sit at the feet of those who have replaced us at the center of religious affections among increasing numbers of people. The conservative Christian movement has within it certain values we would do well to investigate, if not adopt. Among them are the following four:

Knowledge. Often these brothers and sisters appear to be far more profoundly informed about their faith than are those on the rolls of most of our mainline churches. They know and can quote their Bibles. They spend many hours each week in serious study. They can articulate the content of their faith because they have a grasp on what it is. While their theology might be strained and truncated, they are seldom unprepared "to make a defense to anyone who calls you to account for the faith that is in you." While they may not always do it with "gentleness and reverence" (1 Peter 3:15), the grasp of what they have been taught far exceeds that of many mainline church members.

Commitment. While there may not be significantly greater numbers of fundamentalists than mainliners in any given community, when the doors of the churches are open the evangelicals are more likely to be inside. If these congregations seem to have almost limitless financial resources for the world mission as well as for local needs, it is because tithing is taken seriously. If the secular world often preempts the time and energies of mainline Christians, evangelicals seem less affected by the incursion of commercialism.

Many of the fundamentalists I have talked with don't worry about whether the Little League gears up on Sunday mornings, or whether that is the best time to shop, or take to the lake, or play golf. Their priorities are clear. If it interferes with religious commitments, it takes a back seat.

During one of my sabbaticals I spent time in the Orthodox monastic communities of Mt. Athos, where the values of the committed, disciplined Christian life were graphically spelled out. For more than a thousand years monks of various Eastern orders have worked and prayed in this isolated and totally unworldly peninsula jutting into the Aegean Sea from the coast of northern Greece. I discovered two very different types of monastic settlements. The first were the "ideorhythmic" houses. The word comes from two Greek roots which, loosely translated, mean "doing your own thing at your own pace." These monks often had their own funds, private apartments, and occasionally even servants. They participated in the monastic cycles of prayer and work at their leisure. Discipline was almost nonexistent, and the word of the "Igumenos" or abbot had little effect on anyone. The members of these liberal communities were often slovenly, and their buildings universally in a state of disrepair. The gardens were poorly tended and the ancient libraries unused. These monasteries were inhabited by a handful of unkempt old men, who didn't seem committed to much of anything.

Other communities were made up of "cenobites." These orders were highly disciplined, profoundly structured, and under the strict rule of the Igumenos. All possessions were held in common. The residents tended to be young men, who were clean, bright-eyed, and interesting. Only in these conservative communities did I find monks ready to discuss their faith. Recently completed murals adorned the walls. The gardens were well tended, and pilgrims were graciously received. While the theology was excruciatingly narrow—they still wanted to debate the use of the *filioque* clause—and while they excluded me from entering their chapels during their various liturgical acts, they knew their Bibles and the meaning of their faith. The ideorhythmics appeared to be slowly dying relics of a long-gone past. Unless hit by a fresh reformation they cannot survive for long. The cenobites, on the other hand, were vital, generative, and future-oriented.

To the extent the mainline and the evangelical churches of our day are in turn ideorhythmic and cenobite, the future belongs to the latter. The issue seems to center around the capacity of the mainline churches to recover a sense of discipline and commitment without buying into an arcane theological system. Can liberals find again powerful forms of commitment, or does a profoundly effective faith inevitably rest on such doctrines as the inerrancy of scripture and the exclusive claims of those who believe it? Can discipline exist in a community that rests on a foundation of freedom? These are among the serious questions we must subsequently address.

Spirituality. While the quest for spirituality has been at the core of most religious movements, among conservative Christians this quest has become a cultivated phenomenon. For charismatics, spirituality begins in a fascination with what is called "the gifts of the Spirit," the primary evidence being the ability to speak in "heavenly" tongues or languages. These and other gifts form only the facade of what is often an inner hunger for God and for communion with God. At best they may give evidence of a deep and abiding prayer life, an immersion in the Bible and its message, a passion to find a peace that defies understanding, and a thirst to discover God at the center of what is real. Spirituality may be seen in concerns for healing and wholeness of the body and the spirit. It pays attention to the inner voice, to meditative skills, to a separation from the world and its vulgarities. Spirituality is centered on discovering the deep that calls to deep. Yet, while seeking to find the core of being in the spiritual disciplines, many evangelicals, particularly charismatics, have found a profound relationship between body and spirit. Inner feelings often spill over into outer manifestations. Sometimes these inner passions are evidenced in dance, in joyful and fulsome singing, in hands lifted to God, in a vocal response to what is said or done in worship, in embraces and spontaneous words of assurance.

There is a biblically rooted baptism of or in the Holy Spirit, not related to exotic gifts, but to the generic meaning of the Greek word *baptisma*, which means "overwhelm, consume, inundate." This baptismal phenomenon is evidenced in the inner conviction that one's life is in God's hands, and that what is holy is at the center of being. It is demonstrated not so much by the charismatic gifts of the Spirit but by the overflowing of spirituality known as the fruit of the Spirit:

"love, joy, peace, patience, kindness, generosity, faithfulness, gentleness, and self-control" (Galatians 5:22–23a).

Family values. In an effort to fight off the more offensive and narrowly defined aspects of evangelicalism, many mainline Christians may have too easily sluffed off traditional family values. In order to affirm the integrity of a wider variety of lifestyles, we have been hesitant to affirm the more traditional meaning of "family." Where parents and children jointly share a common dwelling, there may be gifts and graces not always found in other settings. Nevertheless, the traditional family may not even constitute the living situation for most of those in our congregations. There are widows and widowers, the divorced, single parents, and singles without children. There are those of the same sex who share committed affectionate relationships, unmarried heterosexual couples with and without children, and those who live in homes occupied by more than one nuclear family. There are communities of faith in which child rearing is the task of the extended family. With an increase in the number of families where both parents work outside the home, parenting occasionally moves beyond absentee mothers and fathers and becomes the shared responsibility of friends and neighbors. Nevertheless, the evangelical commitment to a disciplined life of the traditional nuclear family, centered around the church and its wider notions of clan, is a value not to be brushed off lightly.

While many facets of fundamentalism not only are of little value but should be viewed negatively, the four mentioned earlier—knowledge, commitment, spirituality, and family values—may have at their roots an authenticity not always affirmed or practiced among many mainline denominations and congregations and their more liberal constituents. In later chapters we will see the implications of affirming these attributes throughout the educational, liturgical, and interpersonal aspects of the life and programs of mainline churches.

The Gifts of Secularity

It is no doubt easier for mainline Christians to accept the gifts of secularity, science, and technology than it is to admit that fundamentalists have discovered anything worth emulating. For several years, the congregation I pastored included in its yellow pages ad the following:

> **BRING YOUR MIND TO CHURCH**
> There is no need to park your mind at the church door. Serve and celebrate with us without having to squeeze your beliefs into our mold. At First Christian we are committed to a peaceful world and a just society. A warm welcome, an ecumenical spirit, and a biblical challenge await you.

This ad pointed to a worshiping body of thoughtful people who took the modern world seriously. Gone would be the structures of a faith immersed in superstition. Literary criticism had replaced bibliolatry. An openness to those who were different had replaced the all-too-prevalent sectarian spirit that otherwise dominated the religious life of the city. History, literature, science, philosophy, other religious traditions, and the arts were welcomed as friends and colleagues.

As a marketing tool this ad, and others of a similar strain, were only marginally successful. The midwestern community of 75,000 had already defined religion as something very different. Fundamentalist churches were falling all over each other to see who could build the largest auditoriums as well as control the local government, the schools, and the social ambiance. While evangelicals continued to press openly an agenda focused on such issues as prayers in the public schools, abortion, the exclusion of homosexuals from the mainstream, and the teaching of creation science, our congregation openly affirmed quite a different set of convictions. While making friends with unrighteous mammon and not only accommodating but celebrating the modern world, the question arose as to whether the coalition was too comfortable. We will presently examine the downside of this cozy relationship.

Reform movements within the church have not always been reactionary. Many earlier efforts at church reform attempted to relate Christianity to rationalism—the precursor of secular scientism. Petrarch, a fourteenth-century "humanist," sought to apply the values and lessons of antiquity to questions of Christian faith and morals. Erasmus of Rotterdam devoted his energy to bringing about a reconciliation of what had become a superstitious religious world with both the antiquities and the scholarship of his day.

At the dawn of the Reformation, Martin Luther espoused literary criticism. He realized that the Bible needed to be available in the language of the people. Luther did not view the Bible as level, with every section being of equal importance to faith. No book or passage was to be accepted without critical reflection. He called the book of James "an epistle of straw." Many other reformers had little use for the superstition that had engulfed the church.

A number of churches that grew out of the Reformation tended to affirm the relationship between faith and higher education. The secular disciplines stood alongside theological and philosophic disciplines as the marks of an enlightened and educated clergy. Harvard, Yale, and later Princeton were testimonies to the seriousness with which this relationship was pursued.

Beyond these prestigious academies, every mainline denomination spawned a string of colleges scattered across the plains and mountains of North America. I attended such a school, set amid the wheat fields of Oklahoma, whose motto read "Christian Education Is the Hope of the World."

Both in Europe and in the United States new interpretive tools produced by science became accepted by biblical scholars. Thus the rise of critical theories about the origin and interpretation of the Scriptures. When the natural sciences began to theorize about the origin and age of the earth, a liberal religious community celebrated these findings as expanding our notions of the greatness of God. While science explored the creation of the world, the church affirmed that, no matter the *when* or the *how*, the *who* was God.

As the social sciences developed—sociology, psychology, political science—enlightened church men and women rethought the developing implications for the gospel. The gospel had to do with the values and integrity of human life quite apart from anything remotely related to some other world. Among the important contributions made by the bishops of England was their insistence that a sewer system be built under the streets of London.

Even if we see it as no more than a corrective to an anti-human and corrosive sectarianism, secularity, and its vigorous rationality, can be an ally. While we cannot swallow secularism wholesale—it remains the biggest threat to authentic faith—there are many things we have to learn and adopt from the world that exists far beyond our parochial borders.

The Resistant Agenda
Fundamentalism

While we not only recognize but also accept and celebrate the values and gifts of our two antagonists, fundamentalism and secularity, we do not make an easy peace with either.

Fundamentalism is wrong about the Bible, wrong about history, wrong about science, and ultimately wrong about the grace of God. Fundamentalism is legalistic and judgmental. It attempts to define people out, instead of serving a Lord who defined the outsiders in. My colleague Walter Reed III holds that heresy is anything that attempts to limit the grace of God. Fundamentalism is particularly dangerous when it makes common cause with conservative politics. We resist it by being very clear publicly about the content of our faith, and why we believe what we do. When fundamentalists articulate an understanding either of the gospel or of the world that we find abhorrent, we should not hesitate to say so. While we may not win many battles in the public arena these days, staying silent serves no purpose.

In my community, conservative Christians are increasingly bringing pressure on public institutions. At meetings of the local school board they have shown up in large numbers to ward off what is called "Outcome Based Education." This new pedagogic model has as its core the teaching of certain values. It is not that fundamentalists resist imparting values. Indeed, they insist that a culture without commonly held and taught values is doomed. But among the values taught under OBE is the notion that everyone must be treated with respect and accepted for who they are. Since this means gays and lesbians, as well as others outside the mainstream, fundamentalists believe this methodology cannot be allowed in the public schools.

In our community, as in hundreds of others across the nation, the public library has become a battle zone. When the library purchased and displayed a sex manual for gay men, the evangelical community erupted. Thousands of signatures appeared on petitions, and scores of angry citizens attended meetings of the library board. With modest help from members of mainline churches, the board held firm and the effort to have taken from the shelves books that did not meet the fundamentalist litmus test was resisted. The battle has now moved to city hall where nominees for public boards and agencies originate. In local elections, "stealth candidates" have already arisen. Left unchallenged, fundamentalists may well take over local government as well as the cultural and educational institutions that have long been the backbone of the rational life of the community. The mainline church dares not sit quietly by and allow this to happen.

Beyond these public matters, mainline churches are being tempted to mimic what seems to work for evangelicals. Altars are being replaced by sound stages, and sturdy liturgical styles jettisoned for worship that is more entertainment than devotion. Every mainline pastor has been visited by at least one depressed member of the flock insisting that "if it works [which means, draws crowds], it must be right." Turning mainline congregations into pale reflections of local, popular, nondenominational mega-churches is a testimony to despair, not to hope. Where fundamentalists have something to offer, we need to listen. But where they, for the sake of success, have dispatched what we believe to be authentic faith, we must openly and vigorously resist.

Secularism

As we must resist fundamentalism, we must also be wary lest we succumb to the siren sounds of a secular culture. MTV is not a testimony to the coming of God's reign.

Science is not our shepherd. There are some sacred things that must not be vulgarized. Not every sexual expression merits our blessing. Marriage is not to be viewed as the least acceptable living arrangement. The accumulation of things is not the end product of the fulfilled life. Toys and gadgets are not ultimate. A generation that has forgotten the story of Jesus and his love gives no evidence that humankind has matured.

When it appeared that the people of God were being swallowed by a virulent secularism, King Josiah discovered, or produced, an ancient book that retold his people's most important story. Without that story Josiah believed they could not survive. At the heart of this document were the words:

> When the LORD your God has brought you into the land that he swore to your ancestors, to Abraham, to Isaac, and to Jacob, to give you—a land with fine, large cities that you did not build, houses filled with all sorts of goods that you did not fill, hewn cisterns that you did not hew, vineyards and olive groves that you did not plant—and when you have eaten your fill, take care that you do not forget the LORD, who brought you out of the land of Egypt, out of the house of slavery. (Deuteronomy 6:10–12)

Every advance in science is not a gift of God. Hiroshima, while a testimony to the marvels of technology, is not to be celebrated, and an image of the mushroom cloud does not belong in our sanctuaries alongside the cross. When Thoreau heard that a railroad was to be built near Walden Pond, he wondered if it wouldn't amount to little more than evil going faster.

We cannot retrieve Sundays as a day set aside by our society for religious purposes and rites. However, when the Little League decides to play its games on Sunday mornings, it is time for mainline church families to say, "Our sons and daughters will not be present." Far too many children brought up in churches where they learned not only Bible stories but also liberal values have wandered into secularism, untouched by the demands of faith. Too many of our grandchildren have Santa Claus, not the manger child, as the center of the Christmas celebration. Indeed, often the babe no longer even makes an appearance as a minor character.

A world totally committed to secular values, stories, traditions, and perspectives is not a world for which we can or should pray. There is more to Sunday mornings than good coffee and the *New York Times*, or the weekly trip to Wal-Mart. Once we lose the stories and traditions of faith and are content to live in fine large cities that we did not build, the next generation will lose the values that are the products of the stories they no longer remember and can no longer tell. Few of their children will want to live in a society without religious symbols, artifacts, institutions, rituals, traditions, values, or persons. But that is exactly the sort of community secularism promises. At this writing the masses of people who have graduated from liberal religious institutions into secularism have sown seeds from which will come bitter fruits.

The Humble Agenda: Accepting Mortality

While affirming the rightness of what we have been and are, the mainline church must also recognize the mortality of much of what has been precious in the past. It may be that our day reached its peak some years ago, and after a slow decline, churches like ours will die, opening the way for that which is new and fresh.

Mainline religion came into being as the product of a particular culture. Insofar as it is tied to that culture, it rises and falls with it. All religion is contextual—that is, it bears a specific interpretive relationship to the culture in which it lives. When that culture is eclipsed, its institutions, including the religious ones, die with it. We may be at a startling new point in Christian history. If the first Christian millennium was essentially the period of what might be called the Eastern Church, the second Christian millennium has been dominated by the Western Church—Roman Catholic and Protestant. But radical changes are at hand. Already the vast majority of Christians no longer live in Europe and North America, but increasingly in Latin America, Africa, and Asia. The third Christian millennium may belong to the Southern and Asiatic regions of the world.

Likewise, a theology rooted in neo-Platonic Western philosophy will not long survive in a world where that way of thinking no longer pertains. (For a more complete explication of this point you may want to see my *Building a Biblical Faith*.)

Only our acceptance of the graciousness of God is sacrosanct. Ways of organizing congregations and groups of congregations, forms of worship, styles of music, the relationship between clergy and laity, denominations, ecumenical bodies, theological education, social witness, and missions will all undergo extensive modification—in fact already are doing so. Some of these time-honored ways of being may indeed become no more than historic curiosities. The era of the Protestant denomination may be coming to an end. We must be prepared to let go what is no longer serviceable in the work of God's coming reign. Churches that formerly understood missions as sending folks to the great masses of the unconverted may find that missions will mean receiving workers from former client churches. Already the congregation I served has received a missionary pastor from the church in Indonesia.

At this point we do not know what will die. But clearly many of the long-familiar, cherished structures and forms will not make it very far into the next century.

Often the vast majority of medical resources are spent on the last few months of a patient's life. It would be bad stewardship and bad theology to exhaust our resources keeping the ecclesial patient on life support as she slowly expires, when resources are desperately needed elsewhere. Even if the mainline church endures, many of the things that have been important to it will not. Faithful wisdom lies in letting die that which cannot be saved or which has outlived its usefulness in the cause of God's coming reign.

The Generative Agenda: New Wineskins

The remaining chapters of this book will largely center on how the mainline church redefines its function and develops fresh tools for a new historic moment.

> New occasions teach new duties,
> Time makes ancient good uncouth;
> They must upward still and onward,
> Who would keep abreast of truth.
> —James Russell Lowell

We have long known that the banner hanging over the chancel of dying churches reads, BUT WE HAVE ALWAYS DONE IT THIS WAY. Nevertheless, we habitually replicate what has been without much thought as to whether it is still valid. If there is to be a new day for the mainline church, a new generative agenda must emerge, and that means new wineskins. To that creative enterprise we will now turn.

Questions for Reflection and Discussion

1. If there are cycles in history, religious and secular, that move from liberal to conservative and back again, where are we at the present moment, and how is church life affected?

2. On pages 30–31 there appears an extended mission statement, which is the heart of the thesis advanced in this book. Consider each section of the statement. How could these sections be reworded or revised to articulate where your congregation might best find its work and purpose?

3. If the life and work of the church must grow out of what it believes, what place does theology—the articulation of what we believe—have in your congregation? Are your congregants theologically rooted? How is this rootage lived out? What are the specific programs in your congregation that call for the deepening of a faithful understanding of the Christian gospel?

4. Consider the four things we may have to learn from our fundamentalist brothers and sisters: knowledge, commitment, spirituality, and family values. List the specific ways your congregation might build these concerns into its life and work.

5. We live in an age in which people want to be told what to think rather than be helped to think through important matters for themselves. In some circles intellectualism has become a despised word. How is the life of the church rooted in what it believes, and how are members of your congregation confronted with the task of "giving a reason to anyone who asks for the faith that is in them?"

6. Is "Christian humanism" an oxymoron?

7. If the fundamentalists are the truly successful religious practitioners in our era, why not simply discover the formula for their success and copy it?

8. Does the time ever come for institutions, including religious ones, to die gracefully? How do you know when to let go?

4 | The Theological Imperative and the Work of the Minister

At its heart the church must be an institution rooted in theology. When it is vital, the church stays focused on what it believes and how that faith enables it to understand and call to reconciliation the world in which it lives. When what the church does flows from other than what it believes, religion is either ineffective or dangerous. It is not to be inferred that the average church member was or should have been expected to be a sophisticated academic theologian. Children, long accepted as important parts of the community of faith, are received without passing intricate theological examinations. The grace of God does not depend on one's ability to articulate the content of the faith. Nevertheless, life inevitably flows from one's major commitments. Theology is inextricably tied up with doing the truth. But to do the truth one must understand what the truth is and why it is truth.

The Decline and Fall of Evangelism

In its earlier centuries greater efforts were made by the church to be certain new Christians were equipped with the rudiments of theology. Indeed these learners, or catechumens, were not welcomed to the consecration of bread and wine—the Eucharist—until they not only knew but could verbally defend what they believed. One of the earliest non-canonical books, the *Didache*, was essentially a manual of doctrine and discipline for catechumens.

In all three major branches of Christianity—Roman, Eastern, and Protestant—more than occasional attention has been given in recent times to the preparation of candidates for baptism. Often these budding Christians have been younger children or adolescents who were guided through what became known as confirmation classes. After instruction, those who were baptized in infancy *confirmed* the vows made earlier on their behalf. Those who were not baptized as infants were offered similar instructions by pastors (or those assigned this responsibility) and were subsequently baptized upon their own confession of faith.

With the coming of revivalism this rational instruction did not always take place. Persons deciding to confess their faith responded to an invitation offered after preaching. More than occasionally this was a heartfelt emotional response, or one generated by somebody else's expectations. Those coming forward *may* have been well prepared ahead of time, but in many cases they were not. Children as young as five and six were encouraged to receive Christ as their personal Savior. Whether children or adults, the important issue was the experience and the decision. Understanding was not an essential element. Thus congregations became more and more populated with members who were warm of spirit but short of preparation.

Among some mainline churches better marketing became a hallmark of institutional success. Too sophisticated for the emotionalism of revivals, carefully honed visitation efforts often produced amazing results. Early in my ministry I received 137 persons into the church on a single Sunday morning. It was the end of a weeklong visitation effort held under the guidance of a nationally recognized expert in evangelism. We had set a goal of 135 new converts. By Saturday night we had only 133 signed up. The evangelist and I spent the evening in a nearby apartment building where we knocked on doors—cold calling! After some time we finally encountered four people in one unit who were willing to listen to us. We first suggested we were making a religious survey. Picking up on clues the four offered, the evangelist finally said, "We are here to witness for Christ and against communism. How do you stand?" Having agreed with us that Christ was good and communism bad, we had them sign a card and counted them in the total announced the next morning. I never saw fifty of those people again, and at the mass baptism, in which about forty went under the waters, I couldn't even recite their names. On Monday morning, faced with this thick stack of cards, I wept.

In increasing numbers of mainline congregations, people could be bigots, idol worshipers, or anything else, but when they responded to the invitation or signed up, they got listed in the annual report. They often came down the aisle "just as I am," and left just as they were. Among certain Baptists the only protection the church had was a procedure by which people were not officially part of any local congregation short of a positive vote by that body.

More recently, mega-churches and others have conducted sophisticated surveys to see what products the market wanted and have designed church programs to meet emerging needs. More will be said about evangelism in Chapter Eight.

The Dilution of Theology

Theology increasingly became a bad word. It was something that eggheads in seminaries did. It had little relevance and generated even less interest in most evangelical congregations. A suspicion arose that theologians were all heretics, and readily substituted human opinions for what the Bible said. Even if the parish minister wanted to be invested in this rational discipline, there was no time. Caught reading a book other than the Bible, the local clergyperson would often be tempted to slide it under the desk at the approach of a leading layperson.

The problem was exacerbated as congregations became less and less centers of faith and more and more social units within their communities. It was here that like-minded friends gathered to enjoy food, fun, and fellowship. Programs were piled on programs until the average church member could be in the building or engaged in a church activity every night of the week. It was a safe place filled with compatible people. While Bible study might have been one of the central foci of all this activity, there were probably fewer engaged in that discipline than were quilting, bowling, jogging, doing yoga, dieting, learning how to be parents, serving on committees, singing in choirs, or any one of a thousand other activities. It must not be assumed that any of these programs were irrelevant. Every one of them had a place in the broad repertoire of modern church life. People chose certain churches depending on to what extent their social needs were being met. However, the occasional class in theology, church history, or any of the related disciplines was rarely the best attended activity.

Happily, the well-documented blurring of denominational lines often derailed the more strident forms of sectarianism. But among mainline churches, what one held as matters of faith had little to do with what congregation or denomination to which allegiance was given. This further dilution of religious fervor meant that no longer was it necessary for the average member to articulate a faith stance over against those of other religious bodies. One didn't need to know for what one's church stood. Since "we're all going to the same place," any statement of faith was as good as any other. Churches were really interchangeable social groups; it was not a matter of great moment how faith was to be understood. The situation was exacerbated by a strident anti-intellectualism that pervaded American culture.

The Role of the Mainline Minister

Consider the role of the parish minister, given the emerging nature of congregational life. What are the expectations placed on local pastors? How do they understand the task? There are fewer more complicated assignments than those placed on parish ministers.

While different historic epochs have emphasized different ministerial models, ordination has always been to a multidimensional calling. Ronald Osborn, in his book *Creative Disarray* (Chalice Press, 1991), defines a dozen different models for ministry that have appeared at one time or another in the history of the church. He suggests that during the earliest Christian centuries the clergy were primarily teachers of religion. Priests catechized neophytes in the basics of the Christian faith. Bishops defined and defended orthodoxy, and were primarily teachers and shepherds. Awakeners and revivalists called people to faith through preaching. Meanwhile, the laity assumed responsibility for the organizational and missional aspects of church life. In the book of Acts, seven men were assigned the administrative and pastoral task of seeing that the needs of Jerusalem's Hellenistic widows were met, so that the apostles could devote themselves to "prayer and to serving the word" (Acts 6:4).

With the bureaucratization of the parish, these didactic functions were eclipsed by what Osborn identifies as a managerial style. Parish clergy were employed to run institutions, small businesses, competitive enterprises. The minister's value depended on how well the statistical indices of the institution looked. Ministers became administrators, chief operating officers, business managers. Indeed, the life of congregations began to be refocused around structures, committees, and ways to get the work done. Interviews for positions in congregations and even judicatory offices no longer centered on matters of faith, but on how well the candidate could run an organization. During an era in which mainline religion was popular and churches needed to be built, it probably took someone of considerable managerial skills to handle the plethora of detailed work required to make a parish go. Budgets escalated, and construction enterprises needed to be overseen. A minister had to know how to read a spreadsheet and keep a budget in decent repair. In the competitive world a minister had to be adept at marketing so that the congregation got at least its share of the new folks who were joining mainline bodies in considerable numbers. The minister no longer maintained a study. It was now called the "office."

Osborn puts it this way. "The mark of the holy...tends to evaporate from the brow of the Manager, except as transcendent symbols and rhetoric are co-opted to serve programmatic ends. The minister's style imitates the well-known manner, dress, and vocabulary of the secular executive, and nothing about it necessarily points toward God" (145).

At one time the minister might have been the only educated member of a small community. But that day has long since passed. Having lost their status as the intellectuals of their cities and towns, the prestige of ministers was often maintained by a growing sense of professionalism. New professional degrees were now awarded, and ministers stood alongside physicians, lawyers, dentists, and architects as members of the professional class. While never achieving the same salary status of these others, ministers pushed for, and in many cases obtained, somewhat higher places in the economic pecking order.

Ministers were also increasingly called upon to do counseling. This role was more than attending to the pastoral needs of parishioners in crisis, and far more than visiting hospitalized parishioners.

Certain technical psychological skills were now required. Most ministers took at least one quarter of advanced training in pastoral counseling or clinical pastoral education. The first year out of seminary I spent two days a week in such a program at St. Elizabeth's Hospital in Washington, D.C. Those hours immeasurably enriched my entire ministry. At various times since then I have spent ten to twenty hours a week helping troubled people sort through the trash and the treasures of their lives.

With the coming to the fore of what was called humanistic psychology, more and more of these pastoral hours were consumed in encounter groups and other forums of the increasingly popular human potential movement. Summer enrichment weeks were as likely to be spent at Eslen as at a seminary. The aim was to help people be themselves. Ministers were available to enable folk to feel less guilty, not to reflect, teach, or lead to faith. Religion was restricted to helping folks be happy, think well of themselves, and find peace of mind.

Pastors were also consumed with what was going on in their communities, and could be numbered among the activists and change agents. Led by the example of Dr. Martin Luther King, Jr., the civil rights movement was peopled by those who bore the marks of ordination. In his wake were numbered ministers from most American cities and towns. During the Vietnam war many religious leaders became the conscience of the nation. Beyond that, new organizations were developed that were dedicated to the alleviation of hunger, homelessness, and other forms of human suffering.

As denominations increasingly became bureaucratic structures requiring enormous amounts of time, energy, and money, parish ministers offered them long hours in support of the important work of the church beyond the congregation.

In a sense, all of these consuming functions grew in rich theological soil. But they were often rootless, related to activity but detached from meaning. In an effort to tie these enterprises together, seminaries developed divisions dedicated to the study of "practical theology."

Gradually, however, at the level of the congregation the reasons for doing the work of Christ were eclipsed in the doing itself. The burgeoning of these multifaceted functions slowly squeezed the minister out of the historic roles of theologian and teacher. Instead of equipping the saints for their work of ministry, ordination became the doing of what was rightfully the work of the whole church. Most parish ministers no longer saw themselves as theologians, and would quickly deny any accusation to the contrary. Theologians were a rare breed who lived in seminaries and graduate schools. The minister lived in the real world of committees, services, boards, budgets, and professional responsibilities.

Redefining the Role of the Minister

The question before us is this: Given the times in which we live, how shall we redefine the role and function of the ordained minister? It is my position that both parish and extra-parish clergy must again become theologians, teachers, and servants of the Word. We have within our congregations a great variety of people who can and ought to do many of the tasks ministers have taken over—or have been left with. Few congregations are without men and women who can design budgets and run programs. Every modern farmer must be part businessperson, and is therefore fully capable of handling the financial affairs of most congregations. Other competent people can plan fellowship programs, arrange class schedules, operate food kitchens, halfway houses, and shelters for the homeless.

On the American frontier, where there were few settled ministers, the layfolk of the parish did everything—including, in most cases, the performance of the liturgical functions. When ministers got tired of riding from place to place on horseback and found it more comfortable to settle down in one community, this "settled clergy" gradually took over most of the tasks that had previously been performed by lay members of congregations. In community after community there were battles for institutional supremacy between the congregational "elders" and the settled clergy. The clergy most often won these battles, partly because they could spend full time fighting them, and partly because they simply assumed clerical authority. Increasingly, they were backed up by the clout exercised by judicatories and denominations. The laity quietly took their places in the pews and became an audience. If ministers subsequently began to feel overwhelmed by the variety of tasks placed on them, they had asked for it.

The Theological Imperative and the Work of the Minister 53

Obviously any serious attempt to alter this system will be met with shock and resistance. One cannot just make an announcement at a board meeting or from the pulpit. "After all, don't we pay our minister to run the church?" If, however, the fundamental task of the minister is to be theologian in residence, perhaps the best place to begin is in developing a didactic process in which the roles of minister and laity are redefined. The congregation must be led through the process the task force at St. Paul's took on (as outlined in Chapter Two). Calling and equipping the body to discover new models of church life may be the initial imperative placed on the minister who is concerned about redefining the nature of parish life. I suggest that this is a matter of theology, not simply one of administrative function or process.

If the programmatic, administrative, and financial affairs of the parish are returned to the laity to whom they rightly belong, not so the theological or educational task. The minister needs to be prepared to spend as much as six months in extended conversations with the task force before the organizational work is taken up. In the meantime, the normal functions of church life need to continue almost as is. The usual program does not come to a halt while the new process is taking shape.

Raising false expectations, or allowing the group to replicate once useful patterns, will ensure little that is ultimately creative is likely to happen. We have all been through carefully orchestrated efforts to assist a committee, agency, business, or community board redefine its mission and determine its program.

The most popular exercise is what has been called the SWOT program: "Strengths, Weaknesses, Opportunities, Threats." Small groups brainstorm each of the four concerns, and their lists are placed around the room on large pieces of newsprint. The whole body then distills the suggestions into a single mission statement with attached major objectives and accompanying program goals. While often useful, this organizational development design is not what I am suggesting. I have been through this exercise with a number of congregational groups. The results are most often predictable—you come out just about where you went in.

The limitations of this and similar group processes have to do with the lack of fresh information or insights that get built in at the outset. Everybody knows that the membership needs to be increased, more attention given to finding young families with children, developing a better youth program, improving the music, providing a friendlier environment, expanding the financial resources, keeping the building in repair, caring for the needs of the older members, etc., etc., etc. While these objectives are admirable, those who develop them may be oblivious to the realities with which most mainline churches now must live. The predictable conclusions reflect an old paradigm suitable to an age no longer with us. They are overloaded with dated thinking.

What we are suggesting cannot be done on a Saturday afternoon, or even at a weekend retreat. Nothing happens before the group is taken through a careful examination of the materials such as those detailed in the first three chapters of this book. Unless people know where they are, they will have no idea what direction they ought to go. Obviously a radical departure will unnerve the traditionalists in our congregations. But left to the traditionalists, these congregations will die slowly.

The minister has now assumed the fundamental role as a teacher of religion—or theologian in residence. Slowly the rest of the life and work of the congregation is reassigned to others. New leaders emerge. People on the periphery are drawn to the center. The church begins to redesign its administrative machinery and clarify the essential parts of its mission.

Lay Theologians and the Smaller Congregations

In the foreseeable future the vital mainline church will probably be more compact and its members more theologically literate than they have been for some time. While the minister will be the theologian in residence—indeed that will be the basic task—the entire congregation will take on a new religious intensity. Later we will talk about how this image is reflected at a variety of points in the church's life, witness, and program.

It is obvious to anyone who looks that if solid, or formerly solid congregations, such as St. Paul's, are in trouble, how much more profound are the problems facing smaller, marginal congregations. This is particularly true in those cases where changes in economics and demographics have radically shrunk the communities in which they ministered. Many farm and country towns have all but disappeared. Year after year denominational statistics list the congregations that have run out of people and have been forced to close.

We are long past the time when significant numbers of churches still open can afford a full-time seminary-trained minister. Well-meaning but modestly educated lay leaders from within the congregations, as well as pastors of yoked parishes, have made marvelous and faithful contributions in many places. Nevertheless, multitudes of struggling congregations either limp along doing the best they can, or are easy targets for fundamentalists or ill-educated products of the local independent or sectarian Bible college. Many of these ministers, operating outside the mainline denominational structures, are not as fixated on their professional status and will work for more modest wages than will the typical seminary-trained and properly credentialed cleric. These days the latter are usually carrying a substantial debt for their years in college and seminary, and cannot support a family on a hundred dollars a week and an occasional chicken.

Often denominations have assumed that these smaller struggling congregations can be made into miniaturized replicas of their big sisters. Despite efforts to bolster small churches, they continue to dwindle in size even as they increase in number. If mainline congregations are to be centers of theology and not just social units, how are these bodies to be taught? Who will be the theologians, and how will they be supported?

The question involves how a congregation understands its relationship to other local churches of its denomination, and even beyond its parochial boundaries. Among the free churches in the mainline tradition, one buzz phrase has been "the autonomy of the congregation." This notion resonated positively on the American frontier, but has little relationship to anything we know about the nature of the church. The word "autonomy" comes from two Greek roots, which mean "law to oneself." Yet nowhere in the Scriptures or in the early records of the Christian movement is it suggested that any part of the body of Christ is a law to itself. We are joined to one another, and the head cannot say to the hand, "I have no need of you." Many larger churches, although deeply committed to the functions and administrative work of their denominations, have been independent. They have operated their better-funded ministries and programs almost oblivious to the score of small struggling congregations on the periphery of their communities. If the mainline church is to emerge from its present captivity with any strength, it cannot ignore its smaller congregations. New sorts of relationships must be developed between larger and smaller bodies.

If we have redefined the role of the minister to that of primarily a teacher, then the major administrative and programmatic work of the congregation once more becomes the venue of the laity. This division of labor should release the minister from the myriad of details needed to keep the machinery in repair and operating. One well-educated and competent minister can therefore be the theologian for more than one congregation.

A cluster of smaller churches may form a new organic relationship making use of the "cathedral" for specific services, chief of which would be theological education. Instead of attending two board or committee meetings a week in the congregation, the minister may now be free to spend an evening a week in a teaching ministry with one or more of the smaller churches. Preferably these sessions would be held on location, not in the "cathedral." Smaller churches, often without full-time pastoral leadership, have always known how to operate their own internal programs. What they have lacked is an adequate teaching ministry. As part of this larger enterprise, they should make some financial contribution to the larger church, so that what happens is part of their program. What is received for free—unless it is the grace of God—is seldom helpful.

Obviously, it is difficult for a person to be in more than one place at a time. How shall these smaller bodies be served on Sunday mornings, since we can assume that time of the week will remain the primary occasion for worship? It will happen as a few of these better prepared laypersons become the leaders of worship—that is the preachers—in the neighboring small congregations. Seminary students often serve in marginal congregations near their schools using the model just described. It may be agreed that all the congregations in a particular area are to use the same lectionary readings as the basis for sermons. If the minister meets with these lay preachers for a two-hour session during the week, half the time can be spent reviewing what went on the previous Sunday and the other half spent preparing for next week's message. Those of you versed in church history will realize that this is hardly a new idea!

As the work of the ordained ministry is the equipping of the saints, then the purpose of their teaching is to enable members of the laity to be adequate teachers. The theologian in residence will become a teacher of teachers—always the appropriate model for the work of the church.

The theological teaching the pastor engages in is not just for the private edification of those in the classes. Laypersons under the minister's tutelage become the teachers throughout the rest of the life of the church. Beginning with those who work in the youngest children's class and continuing to the leaders of the most senior group of adults, a new academic standard is set. After an appropriate transition, *all* teachers are trained by the master teacher of the larger congregation. We would not think of turning loose on our public-school youngsters someone who has never been to college. But generation after generation, churches accept and even recruit folks without five minutes of training to help shape the religious life of these same little ones. Is it any wonder that as adults we have to do so much reeducation, helping people unlearn what they picked up earlier? It is my experience that many adults who have left the church have thought that to be a Christian meant one had to believe Noah got all those critters in that boat, or that when the Bible says creation took six days, that ends the discussion. These were the stories they learned from well-meaning but untaught church school teachers.

Not only do these new adequately trained teachers find their places in the wider educational life of the congregation; they work with the minister in the equipping of teachers and other leaders in the smaller churches. But their work is always done under the appropriate supervision of the theologian in residence. At one time old First Church probably spawned many of the struggling smaller churches in the community, or helped provide funds for their rural counterparts. But after getting them going, the close relationship ended. Now the day may have come when lines of fidelity are reestablished so that every congregation, no matter how small, is provided with adequate theological instruction.

Questions for Reflection and Discussion

1. How does your congregation prepare people for membership in the church? What theological assumptions are made when folks transfer their memberships to your congregation? How are children prepared for baptism or confirmation?

2. Are there ways in which membership recruitment and evangelism—two separate functions—are confused with each other?

3. List all the programs, events, activities in your congregation. Which of them are in place to meet social needs, and which to the increase of theological and spiritual substance among the members?

4. Does your minister consider himself/herself a theologian? And how would you define what a theologian is? What are the expectations for members of your congregation to be theologically literate?

5. Make a quick list of all the ways your minister is perceived both within your congregation and in your community. Rank them in order of importance. Where does his/her call to be theologian, teacher of the faith, and biblical interpreter fall? How much time would you say your pastor spends each week in this teaching role?

6. If the church is really a small business, who is going to be the chief operating officer if not the minister?

7. What specific administrative, managerial, programmatic, clerical, and marketing tasks now performed by your minister might members of the laity perform in order to release the pastor to be your theologian in residence? Where would you start to redefine the minister's role, and is such a redesigning even necessary?

8. If you are a member of a small congregation that may not even have a regular pastor, how do you react to the cooperative teaching-pastoral model developed in this chapter? Would it be workable in your situation? If you are in a larger church, how would you feel about sharing your pastor with smaller congregations, using the suggested model?

9. Are there laypersons in your congregation who would be willing to do the work required to become theologically competent? Would your congregation accept their leadership?

What would that be?

5 | The Nature of Faith: From Theology to Praxis

This is not a book about systematic theology. Nor is it a series of lesson plans for a theological course of study that can be replicated in the mainline parish. For that I refer you to my *Building a Biblical Faith*. And yet, I am profoundly aware that *what* we teach is of great consequence. The popular notion that what is important is having faith, no matter its substance, is too frothy and ephemeral to fill the spiritual void with which many of our age live. Faith in faith is not enough. The fundamentalists know this, and they are right! This author has a theological perspective that at heart is profoundly biblical. And yet I believe we must deal with the Bible in ways that may breathe fresh air and offer new hope to many who find traditional methods of dealing with the Scriptures troublesome and inadequate.

Modern Scholarship and Congregational Bible Study

I have often observed Christian education, even in progressive parishes, being conducted as if the past two hundred years of scholarship had never taken place. Ministers have understood that people want their preaching to be biblically based, and by that mean the way the Bible has "always" been presented. Thus many sincere Christians have been stuck with a literal reading that ignores the marvelous insights brought to light since we began to treat the Bible as a living document put together by real people. Nobody ever bothered to tell these parishioners it was not dictated by God, and did not float down from heaven in a soft black cover.

Many Christians have had to put their tongues in the cheeks when it came to Bible study, believing they were supposed to swallow notions whole they knew down deep could not be true. For many years I offered classes in the congregation I served that took the findings of biblical scholarship seriously. Members of the church were asked to participate in the following year-long courses of study:

- An Introduction to the Christian Scriptures
- An Introduction to the Hebrew Scriptures
- Building a Biblical Faith (An Introduction to Christian Thought)

In Chapter Six we will examine how these classes were structured.

Students would attend their first few sessions and issue great sighs of relief at the materials to which they were exposed. They had lived harboring a long series of questions they felt were improper to ask. They never believed that the universe was created in six days, or that there were a literal Adam and Eve. Nor did they really think that the end of the story would take place in a city with gates of pearl and streets of gold. While these questions might have been raised in their own minds, and perhaps with a trusted friend or family member, they were not voiced at church. After all, aren't there certain minimal things Christians are *supposed* to accept without question? Exploring issues of lower and higher criticism, secular history, the meaning of myth, and how culture conditions faith was sunlight in their previously shadowy religious lives. Beyond the Bible, they had struggled with the literal meaning of the great creeds and other forms of faith, but had never seriously verbalized their doubts. Now they were given the opportunity. I cannot tell you how many solid, longtime Christians would come to me after a session in which a passage was demystified, and say, "I have thought that for years, but I didn't believe I could even raise the question; at least not in church."

Seminary-educated ministers knew the great witness of the church in these matters; but many felt intimidated, and therefore kept secret what they had been taught. Not trusting the laity, this secretive game has been played generation after generation. When the mainline church emerges from these years of institutional captivity, it had better be prepared to be honest about the Bible and about the meaning of faith. We can never go back to a level Bible, a superstitious and inadequate reading of the text, and a literalism that cannot be palatable to thoughtful people.

The modern world, with its scientific methodology, tools for literary criticism, archeological discoveries, and global insights, will not return to a world that ignores what God has provided the human mind. The church that is to be cannot think about God in the same way as did the church that no longer is.

Pity the young pastors, however, who come to their first parish eager to transfer all the knowledge soaked up in the past four years into the heads of those who gather before them on Sunday mornings. It doesn't take long to realize that Art, the carpenter, and Sarah, the attorney, are not on the edge of their seats eager to hear the next lecture concerning the difference between the doctrines of Gregory of Nisa and Gregory of Nasianzus. Academic information is not in itself salvific, or even particularly interesting to most people. Thoreau's words remain accurate. "The mass of men lead lives of quiet desperation." It is only as the biblical message takes root in the practical life and at the points of pain of those it addresses that it becomes an instrument of salvation.

Doing Theology in a Double Context

To do theology is not to sit in a class listening to a lecture—not just that. Theology is rooted in experience, not in doctrine. Theology is the way doctrine takes on flesh and blood. Its final act is "doing the truth." Paul Tillich held that theology seeks to answer the questions that life proposes.

Liberation theologians came to realize that for those they served and with whom they shared life, doing theology was profoundly related to daily experience. Gustavo Gutierrez maintained that the real theologians in Latin America were the poor, who struggled to live in a oppressive culture and who understood faith in that context. For them Bible study lay at the heart of the theological enterprise. The Bible came alive, however, only when it became obvious that its authors were often among the pariahs and the marginalized. It was that context out of which they wrote. God had a preferential option for the poor, and that reality was clear to anyone who read the history of the people of Israel and the marvelous stories of and about Jesus. To know God was to know the poor and the captives God had loved. It was in the Bible this love became most evident.

At the same time, the oppressed peoples of Latin American cities and villages saw the texts from the perspective of their own worlds, and realized that there was a parallel between their oppression and that of the peoples of the Bible. It was in this double context that they knew the Bible spoke about them and was the testimony to the God who loved them, stood with them, and willed to set them free. The Exodus story was their story! And so were many other biblical accounts.

There is an enormous risk, however, in trying to understand faith using only the context of another time or another culture. After graciously reading a book I had written in an attempt to interpret liberation theology for middle-class Christians, Gustavo Gutierrez said to me, "Liberation theology is the way the poor see the Bible, and you are not poor." The hard message was that I had to understand the gospel looking through my own cultural lenses.

To examine the text only in the context of the writers—that is, to do classical biblical criticism—ends up in lifeless academics. To approach the text only out of one's own context is to reduce religion to a narrow, self-serving parochialism. It takes both lenses.

Since there are a variety of contexts, there will be a variety of theologies. My context is not the same as that of the desperately poor, and my reading of a text will be profoundly conditioned by the world in which I live. Or perhaps we would be more accurate to say there are a variety of hermeneutical circumstances.

To review: the first context or the first lens is that of the author, or the community out of which the writing came. What did the story mean in the lives of those who first heard it? The answer to that question is the venue of most biblical criticism and research. Now millennia removed from that situation, we must fit another lens into our theological eyepiece. That lens is *our* context. Theological integrity means we must look through both simultaneously. This is what Bonhoeffer meant when he held that the fundamental religious question is, "What is Christ for us today?"

The text comes to life in the experience of those who do the truth, and the truth is seen through the double contextualization provided by our two lenses. The teacher's task is to grind the lenses! The doing of theology is the work of those who look through them! Only when theology gets out of the lecture room and into the experience of the Christian does it move from an academic subject to praxis.

If theology could be reduced to doctrinal statements, then for any given language there could be only one accurate and true articulation, and that articulation needed to be accurately translated into other languages only to demonstrate its universal authenticity. That notion is, in fact, what fundamentalists seem to hold. It is akin to putting proper Western shirts on the "natives."

During the early centuries, when the church was attempting to define the nature of its faith, it did an amazingly powerful job of speaking out of the culture in which it lived. The philosophic world was dominated by classical Greek thought. The revelation of Jesus Christ and the apostolic message were seen through this lens. Significant to the conversations were ways in which Greek notions eventually shaped a full-blown Trinitarian formula, the relationship between the three persons of the Godhead, and the difference between person and essence. The problem is that this particular context became normative, and has tended to define the issues it developed for all time. The Nicene and Chalcedonian formulae became etched in theological stone, and even though our philosophic context is far different, we even today define orthodox faith in those terms. The fact that different cultures understand the gospel in diverse ways is not so much the product of our sinful divisions as it is the nature of the second lens through which we must look. Christopher Morley once said, "A word to the wise is not sufficient if it doesn't make any sense." Neither does the gospel in cultural forms and words foreign to our worldview.

The theological issue centers around how we authentically understand the gospel in the context of those who lived it and wrote about their experience, and at the same time in our own context. We see Jesus through these twin lenses.

We do not, however, live in theological isolation. There is really a third lens which we must add: the long, powerful history of the Christian tradition. The working out of the issues that eventuated in the Trinitarian solution is also part of our history and our experience, and must not be ignored. The great creeds of the church are, after all, our statements of faith. The danger is that we make ultimate what is historically and theologically proximate. We need to stay clear of worship either at the shrine of our culture or that of fifth-century neo-Platonists.

The Practice of Faith

The issue is this: How does the mainline congregation move from theology to praxis? How do the insights obtained from theological reflection and biblical study become vital in the day-to-day lives of those who hear it? The hiatus between these two disciplines is often painfully apparent. In questions of social justice, for instance, one often hears dedicated parishioners explain their perspectives and actions on the basis of notions far removed from their faith. Every social evil from child labor to slavery has been justified by some commonly held political philosophy or economic theory. While occasionally there were Bible snippets recited to prove this or that point, the fundamental reason for a particular position had little to do with the message and meaning of the gospel.

When theology fails to address the issues people struggle with every day, it has become an arcane exercise without power. The following is a sermon that illustrates the relationship between biblical theology and the practice of religion.

HOW CAN WE BE SAVED?

This morning I will violate two of the principal rules of preaching. I will use a text from a source other than the Bible, and I will talk about everything! The text is from Reinhold Niebuhr.

> Nothing that is worth doing can be achieved in one lifetime;
>   therefore we must be saved by *hope*.
> Nothing that is true or beautiful or good makes complete
>   sense in any immediate context of history;
>   therefore we must be saved by *faith*.

Nothing we do, however virtuous, can be accomplished alone;
   therefore we must be saved by *love*.
No virtuous act is quite as virtuous from the standpoint of our friends or our foes as it is from our standpoint;
   therefore we must be saved by the final form of love, which is *forgiveness*.

The question before us is both evangelical and profound. It relates to wholeness, personal and corporate. How can we be saved?

First, salvation begins with hope, not to be confused with optimism. Optimism is a trust that things will be all right for me, but hope is a confidence that things will be all right long after I'm gone. Optimists plant flowers. The hopeful plant trees. To hope is to take an idea whose time has not yet come, and instill it in a child. People say to me, "You waste your breath when you talk about a new ethic and a reign of God on earth that can operate any way but the way the world operates today." But we keep on talking about a Kingdom ethic, the law of love, world peace, the care of mother earth, not because we are optimistic, but because we are hopeful.

At a recent concert the three-year-old boy behind me made it clear what he thought of Beethoven—until my wife shot the parents a glance that would have melted the Greenland ice cap. But there are public occasions when the cry of a child is a song of hope. An old woman died a few weeks ago, and during the memorial service, a granddaughter nursed a great-granddaughter. But the child was fussy and began to whimper. I was moved to tears, stopped, and asked the congregation to listen. For God had given us a gift—a voice of hope. A text flooded over me: "A generation comes and a generation goes, but the word of our God endures forever."

I am always moved when infants are blessed or baptized. I carry them around the church so that everyone can see them. It is more than a sentimental moment. We take these children in our arms and we introduce them to a group of people, many very old, and we say to these infants, "If there is a future for what we believe, it is in your hands," for nothing worthwhile can be achieved in one generation.

In Kurt Vonnegut's *God Bless You, Mr. Rosewater*, Eliot Rosewater, an eccentric do-gooder, is discussing with his wife the birth of twins to a half-witted townsperson named Mary Moody.

"I'm baptizing them tomorrow," he says. "I didn't know you—you did things like that," Sylvia replied. "I couldn't get out of it," said Eliot. "She insisted on it, and nobody else would do it. I told her I wasn't a religious person by any stretch of the imagination. I told her nothing I could do would count in heaven. But she insisted just the same."

"What will you say?" inquired Sylvia. "Oh, I don't know. I'll go over to her shack, I guess, sprinkle some water on the babies and say, 'Hello, babies. Welcome to the earth. It's hot in the summer and cold in the winter. It's round and wet and crowded. At the outside, babies, you've got about a hundred years here. There's only one rule that I know of, babies: Darn it, you've got to be kind.'"

Our hope is not that we can create a kinder, gentler world. Oh, we may nudge it a bit. But babies, we've got no choice but to leave it to you. We've got to rely on you; therefore, we must be saved by *hope*.

Second, we must be saved by *faith* in what transpired before we arrived. Nothing is made whole in an instant. Faith is affirming what others have lived by, acknowledging that we may not have all the answers in our test tubes and laboratories, our philosophic systems or secular wisdom.

While I'm not about to swallow obsolete doctrines, patriarchal, male-dominated, ignorant views of the Bible, fictional miracle stories, mythic pictures of creation, or a second coming in the clouds, I often wonder if in rejecting the wisdom of the past we have thrown out the baby with the bathwater. Perhaps nothing that is true or beautiful or good can be completely captured in our modern notions.

Could it be that we liberals—and I own that brand—have few answers to the profound questions posed by those who hunger for eternal verities? Society needs us not because we happen to believe in the scientific method, but because we have an inner loyalty to something more vital than Arabian oil, stronger than armies, more imperative than majorities. We are to keep moral watch, not by digital clocks, but by eternal values not conditioned by what the morning paper or the evening news has to say.

We may have outgrown forms of old-time religion, but what we have left is an easygoing religiosity that permits anything and stands for nothing. We are reduced to sentimentality. Could it be that so many modern young people don't find much in churches like ours because we don't seem to be able to say about anything, "Here I stand," but rather we twitter, "It might be this, and it might be that"? Perhaps, just perhaps, nothing that is true or beautiful or good makes complete sense in our immediate context of history.

We nonchalant Christians, we tinkerers with faith, we dilettantes who play with ideas, dabble in spirituality, poke at prayer, hold some effete idea about God—what happens to the foundations of our porous religiosity when the storm comes?

We liberals are good at telling others what we don't believe in. We don't believe in this and we don't believe in that. We have pared down faith until all we have left is a ghostly reminder of what was once a great religion. And seeing how few positive convictions we have left, we grow easygoing about everything, and end with mush and froth. And when a crisis crashes in on a soul, a family or a world; when the storm comes and the wind blows and beats upon the house and it falls—what then?

Consider those who "by faith conquered kingdoms, quenched raging fires, escaped the edge of the sword, won strength out of weakness, put enemies to flight." But we who have reduced faith to a casual curiosity committed to nothing wonder why we win no victories, enforce no justice, put no armies to flight, and end up with churches as powerless as warm spit.

Third, we must be saved by *love*. Our age has deified the individual. Looking out for number one is not only the first rule, it is the only rule. But the gospel is clear that we need one another, and we need the institutions, the glue, that binds us to one another. Jesus called twelve and knitted them into the sturdy fabric we call the church. The Christian enterprise is not a collection of individuals each seeking his or her own path to heaven. The church, with all its faults, betrayals, and denials, is love in action. No one needs to remind me how evil the church has been, how responsible for wars and prejudice, the rape of the earth, and the subjugation of women. I know more horror stories than most members of this congregation, because I know more about church history than you do. There may be more goodness outside the church than in it, but without the church, goodness does not easily pass from one generation to another.

There may be justice without courts, but not for long. There may be commerce without banks, but not for long. There may be education without schools, but not for long. There may be law and order without governments, but not for long. There may be values without families, but not for long. And there may be faith without the church, but not for long.

Institutions are not social cages. They are living testimonies that we are bound together. Our institutions are the legal tender of love in the world. Civilization, after all, is a thin veneer over the savage in all of us. I would not want to live in a city without courts, banks, schools, governments, or families. Neither would I want to live in a community without churches. So when someone says to me, "I am a religious person, but I don't need the church," I respond, "Do you know what you are saying?"

Bill Nottingham, the former president of the Division of Overseas Ministries (Disciples of Christ), was in Leningrad on the day the city's mayor turned over the administration of a large hospital to the church. "We give this hospital to the church because the church is where you find more mercy," said the mayor. Who kept the faith alive during the dark years of the Soviet Union? Groups of old women and a few priests. The church is that body of people who, following Jesus, have pledged to be love embodied. With all its warts it testifies that we must be saved by *love*.

In addition to faith, hope, and love, there is a fourth word in the Christian vocabulary that sums up the other three. It is *grace*. Its companion word is *forgiveness*, and its sign is the cross. If our years of stumbling about this planet have any ultimate meaning, it is because we are forgiven, by one another and by God. None of us can survive a week in any relationship that is not based on grace, forgiveness, and the unconditional acceptance of each other.

If I must be perfect for you to love me, I am through, as dead as a doornail, hopeless as garbage. It is only when I realize that I have been forgiven for all my arrogance and greed, all the injury and hurt I have given you, all the cruel things I have done on purpose or unknowingly, that I can live. When I realize that nothing I do, no matter how virtuous I think it to be, looks that way to you, but you care about me nonetheless, I am saved. And the final sign of forgiveness is the cross. For the root of salvation is not that you forgive me, but that God does.

Thus we are set free to live and to love, to be gracious and forgiving in a world that needs mercy more than it needs anything else. We are thus saved, rescued, accepted. For the ultimate secret of the universe is that we are loved, just as we are, every one of us, all the time. How can we be saved? Only by *hope, faith, love,* and *grace*. For:

> Nothing that is worth doing can be achieved in one lifetime;
> therefore we must be saved by *hope*.
> Nothing that is true or beautiful or good makes complete sense in any immediate context of history;
> therefore we must be saved by *faith*.
> Nothing we do, however virtuous, can be accomplished alone;
> therefore we must be saved by *love*.
> No virtuous act is quite as virtuous from the standpoint of our friends or our foes as it is from our standpoint;
> therefore we must be saved by the final form of love, which is *forgiveness*.

Doing the Truth

Several decades ago, what was called the "action-reflection" model was popular among Christian educators. Learning took place not in isolation, but on the road. Whether the ideological understanding or the activity came first seemed beyond the point. One learned by doing and did by learning, and these two disciplines were intertwined.

Others were convinced, however, that action always preceded understanding, and, therefore, a behavioristic model was the most effective entrée to learning. "It is easier to act your way into a new set of feelings—or beliefs—than it is to feel your way into a new set of actions." One comprehended in the doing, not in the intellectualizing.

Under these terms, churches developed multitudes of programs. Christians were expected to dedicate significant amounts of time to a broad range of functions, both within the life of the congregation and in the community. Churches became very busy places. The notion was that subsequently these activists would gather in study groups in an attempt to understand the ways in which what they were doing related to what they believed. As time went on, however, fewer and fewer congregations included the reflection side of the equation. Doing became an end in itself, and the doing drifted far from thoughtful Christian substance. One hardly needs to reflect seriously on a theology for the bowling league or the all-church variety show. Congregations became social units within their communities, dedicated to providing food, fun, and fellowship for folks of all ages and interests.

Under the terms of this action orientation, congregations also did many good things on behalf of the less fortunate. It was generally understood, for instance, that feeding the hungry was an activity in which Christians ought to be engaged. Thus, there sprang up a plethora of food kitchens providing free meals to anyone in need, grocery distribution centers, food banks, "meals on wheels," and a variety of other nutrition programs. Every one of these gracious ventures benefited those who came to depend on them. Rarely, however, did anyone stop long enough to ask the more profound questions. "Why are they hungry?" "How is it that in a land of plenty and opportunity there are more and more people living on the far edge of poverty?" "What is God's will for a society, and how is that will related to Jesus' notion of the kingdom, or reign, of God?" Dom Helder Camara, a bishop of the poorest region of Brazil, once put it this way: "I can spend all day pulling people out of the river, but sooner or later I've got to go up the river to see who is throwing them in." This practicing liberation theologian is also said to have remarked, "When I feed the hungry they call me a saint. When I ask why they are hungry they call me a communist."

While the congregational style centered on the doing often omitted the "why," it was a decided improvement over religionists who would spend countless hours studying the problems of poverty without putting a spoonful of food in anybody's mouth or attacking the root causes for the maldistribution of the world's bounty. Jesus never is recorded to have said, "Blessed are you, for I was hungry and you developed a theology of compassion."

Liberation theologians borrowed from a Marxist analysis the word "praxis" for the simultaneous exercise of doing and understanding. Perhaps it was little more than the reiteration of the action-reflection model. Without reflection, action can become the willy-nilly effort of do-gooders. Without action, reflection can become the effete escape of puffed-up intellectuals.

At another level, most ministers have encouraged their people to pray, often chiding them for the paucity of their spiritual discipline. While some praying may have resulted, there has been an enormous increase in guilt. Many faithful Christians know full well they ought to pray more, but have found that exercise extremely problematic. Intellectually, they can no longer conjure a great listening God, who lives somewhere in the sky and who will rearrange the nature and function of things on earth if "he" is asked to with the proper words uttered often and fervently enough. From time to time, during Lent for instance, or in moments of crisis, an attempt may be made to jump-start a prayer life. The effort may last for a while, but eventually the old, prayerless pattern reemerges. This scenario is not just a problem with the laity. Significant numbers of the ordained—including this author—have found themselves dealing with the same inner conflict.

Often the spiritual discipline of the gathered congregation isn't much better. How many mainline churches still maintain regular prayer meetings or offer opportunities for the broken, wounded, destroyed, and dying to kneel in the midst of the saints and be held in the arms of prayer? It is not that we have gotten out of the habit. *It is rather that we have no theology for that sort of thing.* We have given over the healing enterprise to physical science, on one hand, and to the charismatics on the other. We can complain until we are out of breath about the exploits and the charlatanism of the Oral Roberts and Benny Hinns of the Christian world, but where is the ministry of healing taking place in our churches? It is not that we don't have any time for or interest in the subject. It is that we have no theology to make the activity meaningful.

No longer believing that God will rearrange the forces of nature for our benefit, we are reduced to allowing a variety of twelve-step groups to use our buildings. After all, they still rely on a "higher power," while we are not certain just how powerful this higher One really is. Medical doctors, charismatics, and A.A. groups know what to do. Mainline Christians often do not. And not knowing, we have gradually ceased the attempt. Churches may mention the names of the sick, the grieving, the troubled, and the broken during Sunday morning pastoral prayers. But without an adequate theological base, we no longer find ways to put prayer into action. While we have always known how to talk the talk, walking the walk has not been that easy.

How then do we sustain communities of faith that do the work of Christ and at the same time live out of an understanding as to why they are doing it? How do we inculcate theological integrity into activity? After all, nobody these days has to enter a church to engage in acts of charity and mercy. Nobody has to join a congregation to get involved in a vast assortment of activities for the common good or for intellectual stimulation. If that is what religion is about, you can find secular bodies that are less expensive, devoid of superstitious clap-trap, freer of internal strife, and probably more effective. If you are looking for community and fellowship, try the lodge. If what you need is entertainment with your social peers, there is the country club, the Moose or the VFW. Or, if you want "spirituality" or have need to work on a personal problem, try a twelve-step group.

I doubt if the answer is limited to the expansion of the number of study groups in a congregation. While formal classes do help, the best learning may take place in the context of the doing. What if, for instance, the faithful group that serves at the free-lunch kitchen—in our community it was called The Open Door—stays for an additional hour to reflect not only on what happened that day, but also to take a look at the issues and theological underpinning for the endeavor?

In Chapter Seven you will find the outline of an action-reflection service for healing. This order of service may serve as a model for how the church thinks about the faith and acts faithfully at the same time.

Theology: A Living Encounter with God

While theology is narrowly defined as thinking about God, or literally, "the word (logos) about God," it is not merely an intellectual exercise. Theology is the living encounter with God. In the case of Christian theology, this encounter is not with some far-off heavenly being, but with the God who is with us, in us, around us. To seek God only in the supernatural is to remove God from where God is most alive and real—in the intimacy of day-to-day living, in relationships, in the life of the mind, in acts of mercy and service, in self-sacrificing love. In short, we are found by God and we experience God within history. If Baalism was the worship of a limited nature god, whose domain was confined to a tiny bit of geography, the God we know in the Bible is the God of history, who stands within it.

Religion is an encounter with the God who is the very energy of life; the benevolent power with a purpose we experience most clearly in Jesus. The God of our faith is not an omnipotent being out there somewhere, who is unmoved and unaffected by anything that happens to us. The God we know in and through Jesus shares our history. This God both rejoices and suffers with us. God moves with us and in us, and religion at its best is an intimate relationship with the dynamic One, who is profoundly affected by what happens to us.

The task before the mainline church is clear. If it is to have anything to say or to be when history has moved through this epoch dominated by secularism on the one hand and fundamentalism on the other, strong, theologically alert communities of the faith must be developed. The locus of these centers of faith will primarily be congregations. It is here that the story will be remembered and told. It is here that the songs of Zion will be sung—even within a strange land. It is here that disciples—those who live under a discipline—will not only teach their children the meaning of the Christ event, but will also move from theology to praxis. Even if the current generation dies in Babylon before history turns the corner, its children will go back singing, to rebuild the walls and the temple and to give testimony to the grace and love of the God who will be in their midst.

The issue is how we say powerfully enough to be heard what it means that Jesus is Christ is Lord, and that the reign of God is at hand, without falling into rigid doctrinal statements. How do we confess Christ and what Christ means for us today as did Karl Barth and those who worked with him in the preparation and proclamation of the *Barman Declaration*? Our context is not that of Nazi Germany, and the *Barman Declaration* cannot be our statement. Neither can we adopt as our own the *Kairos Document* developed by Christians in South Africa as they faced the godlessness of apartheid. Our task is to find a way to confess our faith publicly as we confront the particularities and brokenness of our culture in which a few get richer and many get poorer, where racism continues to reign, where selfishness and secularism have been deified, and where nationalism continues to be our religion.

The world does not know what we believe because we rarely say it aloud. The world knows about our doubts, our misgivings, our weaknesses, but it seldom hears these days about our faith. If it wants a clear—or at least a loud— trumpet it must turn to our fundamentalist and charismatic brothers and sisters.

We now move to an examination of several facets of church life, probing specific possibilities for the living out of the gospel. As we do so, we will be cognizant of the options developed by St. Paul's church as outlined in Chapter Three. We will redig some old wells, find what is of value both within our secular culture and within evangelical communities of faith, reject what is invalid, let die what is no longer efficacious, and redefine our mission, using fresh insights and newly honed tools.

Questions for Reflection and Discussion

1. Most Christians have religious questions they are often too embarrassed to ask. What are yours, and in what settings would you feel safe asking them? Do you often wonder about the difference between superstition and authentic faith?

2. Ministers are usually theologically trained. That is, they may know some things about the Bible the average layperson does not. Do you often wish they would let you in on their secrets?

3. Every text was written in a particular period of time out of a particular social situation. What teaching/learning opportunities are there in your congregation for members to discover the kind of world Bible writers inhabited, and what influence would this knowledge have on your understanding of particular texts?

4. What is your context, worldview, or generally assumed philosophic structure, and how does it shape your understanding of the Bible?

5. According to Jesus, faith is not a body of doctrines to be believed, but a life to be lived. Yet the ways we act must flow from those things we hold to be true. What are the religious presuppositions that determine how the church responds to the poor, the hungry, the marginalized, and the outsiders?

6. In the sermon that begins on page 64, there are working definitions of the four key words in the Christian's theological vocabulary: hope, faith, love, and grace. What do they mean to you, and how does each of them determine the ways both individual Christians and the Christian community act?

7. Most congregations are involved at some level in feeding the hungry. How does your congregation go about this task? In what ways does it seek to discover why they are hungry and address those root causes?

8. Read the *Barman Declaration*. (Your pastor should be able to help you locate a copy of it.) What was the historic circumstance that produced this document? If the mainline church today is being squeezed between a political/religious conservatism on one hand and a virulent secularism on the other, how might we articulate our faith in ways that would lead us to more faithful action?

6 | Shaping a Community of Learners

Two generations ago, the congregations of many mainline denominations discovered a new way of doing church administration and program development. Researchers, taking a clue from business, recommended that congregations become organized around commonly identifiable functions that constituted the programmatic core of church life. Most bodies developed a series of functional departments including: evangelism, world missions, Christian social action, stewardship, property, worship and the arts, congregational life, and Christian education. While the terms differed from denomination to denomination, these divisions were basically replicated across the mainline spectrum.

The Demise of the Sunday School

As a way of organizing the work of the congregation, these newly developed programmatic units were far more useful than the prevailing structures dominated by the handful of men variously called the vestry, the church board, the session, or the deacons. These elite bodies often operated autonomously, without much other intra-church structure. In some congregations everything was under the control of the "ruling elder." The new program divisions increasingly became the domain of a more broadly based lay leadership.

This new administrative style, however, did not solve all the problems. One can date the slow demise of the traditional educational life of many congregations with the development of Christian education committees. While not the only reason for the withering of previously powerful systems, the effort to coordinate the teaching-learning functions of a congregation was a body blow to the formerly independent Sunday school. Christian education became the property of an administrative unit responsible to the whole church. The previous owners—dedicated, longtime teachers—were now subject to what looked like an outside committee. The same can be said of the foreign mission emphasis, previously controlled by women's missionary societies, but now operating under the auspices of congregation-wide organizational structures.

Sunday schools, the longtime backbone of the educational program in most mainline congregations, were not initially intended to provide Bible training for the church's membership. They were originally substitutes for secular schools among children who were not afforded the opportunity of even minimal education. So effective was the enterprise that soon this charitable institution began to include the children of church families. In time the venture was metamorphosed into the congregation's Bible school. The program became increasingly popular, and in many congregations the Sunday school competed with worship as the focus of church life. Large adult classes were developed with their own lay preachers. In many cases there was the Sunday school congregation and the worshiping congregation. After Sunday school one could observe a mass exodus. As members of these substantial classes departed, along with other family members, a somewhat different group were showing up for worship. Many churches reported much larger crowds for the former activity than for the latter. Sunday schools developed "opening exercises" to meet the devotional needs of those who never stayed for worship. These twenty-minute services before study time were often complete with orchestras and were usually lay led. Children's classes were taught by long-term, dedicated, Christian women—and occasionally men—who loved the Bible, enjoyed God's little ones, and made lasting impressions during the formative years of growing Christians. Often the theological perspective of these teachers was simpler, more conservative, and folksier than that of the minister. It was not unusual for the teacher of the large Sunday school class to correct what he or she believed to be the wrong religious message emanating from the pulpit.

Ministers often chaffed under the competition. An effort was therefore made to bring the Sunday school under the jurisdiction of the general church program. Thus the development of Christian education committees. Whether it was a matter of causation or correlation is debatable. But the beginning of the demise of large organized Sunday schools occurred simultaneously with this administrative nuance.

History has moved on, and in our day the Sunday school or "church school" crisis is now acute. I have recently heard of a number of churches that have given up on Sunday school altogether. It is not that they decided to dispatch this facet of church life, but that nobody was showing up. The congregation I most recently served had a worshiping congregation of about two hundred. On a good day, Sunday school attendance was fewer than eighty. This count included everyone from the cradle roll to the old-time "Friendship Class"— average age over eighty.

If there is serious trouble in the children's departments of most Sunday schools, the state of things in adult departments may be even more problematic. The large classes have all but disappeared. The demise is a mixed blessing. Often the lessons were semi-sermons delivered by good speakers interested in promoting "the American way." The actual educational impact of passively listening to a lecture, however, is minimal. Again, these "organized Bible classes" were primarily social, not educational, structures. Remnants can be found in shrinking clusters of old friends, who still meet weekly because the other members constitute their primary social group—and have for decades. Lessons often consist in jumping up and down on ten verses, sharing old prejudices, and coming out about where they went in. However, these residual groups are very important and should not be disturbed. They perform a vital function for the saints who attend. Having to give up participation in the class is often the most difficult thing very old people have to do. In addition, these classes are often amazingly good at keeping in touch with their "shut-ins."

In many places Sunday schools are still vital, and to disband them would be a serious error. However, my guess is that it is just a matter of time until they are no more. While their effectiveness in doing Christian education may be coming to an end, those that remain should be allowed to die gracefully. The demise ought to be seen, however, not as an indication that education is less important, but that it is too important to be left to that structure. No one ought to gainsay the dedication of the faithful people who formerly taught classes either of children or the large organized adult constituencies. However, while these folks were long on love and commitment, they were often short on preparation and theological formation.

I fondly remember Auntie Fey, my Sunday school teacher when I was in grades one through three—the Primary Department. A lifelong Bible student, her own religious perspective was limited to a literal reading of the text. The lessons I still recall centered on horror stories from the Old Testament: Daniel in the lion's den, David and Goliath, Gideon's clever slaughter of the Midianites. Eventually I had to unlearn most of what that dear saint instilled in me. Had I never moved beyond Auntie Fey, I would have ended up either out of the church, not being able to swallow the superstition, or as a fundamentalist. Nevertheless, Auntie Fey, and the other dedicated teachers I remember, taught by their lives what I didn't get in their lesson plans.

As denominations subsequently made serious efforts to update the Auntie Feys of the world with a "life-centered curriculum," many Sunday school children were left with little grasp of the biblical text, literal or otherwise. Too often Sunday school became a forum to help little ones understand that Jesus wanted them to share toys. As Sunday schools declined and the Auntie Feys died off, it became more and more difficult to recruit teachers, who all too often were now drawn from the ranks of those willing to show up. Many congregations deployed two or three teachers for every class, because few wanted to commit themselves to being present every Sunday. One church has a rotating teaching staff, where somebody different is present each week of the month. It should come as no surprise that the children in these classes learn practically nothing. While many of those in this new genre of teachers were solid, committed Christians, they were ill-equipped for much beyond the socialization of those in their classes. They had seldom been introduced to solid theological or biblical materials. They did the best they could, however, with minimal resources. God bless them!

While the current epidemic of Biblical illiteracy cannot be wholly laid at the door of the typical Sunday school, it is clearly an inadequate vehicle to do Christian education in our era. At any rate, the day when the traditional Sunday school could carry the weight of the congregation's education program is probably long gone.

Preaching as a Teaching/Learning Tool

A significant number of churches have either supplemented or supplanted their Sunday schools by giving serious attention to other times and formats for Christian education. Historically, Southern Baptists have used Sunday evenings, prior to worship(!), as a time for teachers and learners to gather in serious study. The more liturgical churches, which operate a multi-year catechetical program for children, find the right time to be a weekday afternoon or Saturday morning. What is clear, however, is that if learners show up about half the time and want to play while they are there, it doesn't matter when the session takes place. Nevertheless, what needs to be done cannot be accomplished in forty-five minutes on Sunday morning.

With the shrinking of the average American's attention span, the instructional impact of sermons has drastically changed. A while back, someone in our community suggested that as part of the celebration of the town's one-hundred-fiftieth year, the churches join on Sunday evening in an old-fashioned outdoor service, replicating as nearly as possible an 1845 frontier experience. It never came off for complicated sectarian reasons, but a modest bit of research made it clear that nobody would have tolerated the service had it in fact taken place. Sermons in those days ran two hours, and even then the preacher might just be getting warmed up. And people listened and learned. In fact, the basic theological education for folks on the frontier came from hearing sermons. These days twenty minutes is the maximum, and people like it better when you can pare it down to about twelve! A clever motivational speech, based on a story that makes a point, can be done, perhaps, in twelve minutes. A teaching sermon that moves very far cannot. But when TV producers tell us that about eight seconds is the maximum length of time one can command attention these days, twelve minutes may seem like an eternity.

Not all congregations are in the same place. A few years ago I attended the Sunday morning worship service of an evangelical free church in England. I was prepared for the usual fifty-minute liturgy I had found in the Church of England. The sermon alone, in this crowded auditorium, was almost twice that long! While I shuddered at the theological perspective presented, I was impressed by what I observed. Nobody seemed bored or kept looking at their watches. The sermon detailed a lengthy biblical text, which people followed carefully, as the preacher moved through it. Almost everyone had his or her own Bible, underlining it and making notes in a separate spiral binder. I later discovered that the great majority of these folks gathered in smaller groups later in the week for an hour session to review the same materials with the minister, and to ask questions as to how the text applied to daily life.

It is no secret that most members of the typical evangelical church in North America are far more knowledgeable about the Bible and the substance of the faith than are their mainline counterparts. We just cannot get that kind of commitment. And that may be the root of the problem. Nevertheless, if mainline churches are to become centers of theological literacy, they must rethink the way sermons are handled. Sermons are not entertainment. Rather they provide the minister's primary opportunity to teach.

Commitment: The Key to Survival

If the mainline congregation is simply a pleasant social group, which may adequately address the concerns of folks who need that sort of thing, it may fill definite, albeit limited purposes—as least for now. My guess is that with the multiplicity of social units that can do the same thing, mainline churches maintaining themselves at that level will continue to die out. If that is so, how much has really been lost?

If, however, particularly during this difficult period of captivity, the major task is to build smaller, highly disciplined, articulate, knowledgeable, intentional communities of faith and action that will have something to offer when history cycles around again, then a new look at what those bodies ask of their members is the first order of business. What is obviously called for, a priori, is a reshaping of the educational aspect of church life for adults, youth, and children.

Getting from where we are to the place that sees the emergence of these highly committed church bodies will be a difficult task—many will say, an impossible task. If that is true, then we are stuck with congregations that will continue to lose strength, and denominations that will see decreasing funds, support, and power. Here and there, congregations may show exceptional vitality for a brief time, using the old tools and systems. A powerful minister, just the right location, an innovative program, or some other dynamic may spark them for awhile, but in the long run I doubt if even these will survive. Either we learn how to develop theologically literate, biblically vital groups of laypeople, or we will slowly expire. I believe how we view Christian education, as it is interwoven with the rest of congregational life, lies at the heart of the critical transformation.

The Education of New Members

Consider how we might receive members into these newly committed congregations. While currently the process differs from congregation to congregation, there are certain rather common assumptions and practices. At this point we are not discussing how folks are evangelized, but what happens when they become members of our churches. We will discuss the evangelistic work of the church in Chapter Eight.

What is expected of new members in most mainline churches? For several months immediately following my retirement from parish ministry I visited the worship services of a score of congregations in my community and beyond. Where I could I went anonymously. I found a consistent welcome. The modern mainline church tends to be a very friendly place. I almost always felt wanted. In many of these churches I could have checked on a card I found in the pew that I desired to become a member, and I would have been assured of an immediate call from the pastor, or a visit from a team of laypersons encouraging me to join. Once before, during a time I was in secular work, I worshiped regularly at a mainline church across the street from my apartment. Although I took no part other than to attend the formal service, after three months I discovered in a newly printed church roster that my name was included as a member. When I inquired of the pastor, I was told that members were those consistently present—and that included me. From that day until I left the community a year later, all that was asked of me was a voluntary financial pledge. During the budget campaign I was solicited by a lay couple. It was the only call I ever had from anybody in the congregation. I could have been a serial killer, a child molester, a devil-worshiping cultist, or an outright atheist, and it wouldn't have mattered.

Obviously the newly evangelized, or even those who "transfer in," should not be expected to be mature Christians all at once. They should, however, be expected to enter a disciplined program of study, reflection, and action. Without that commitment at the outset, perhaps membership might not be so quickly offered. A generation ago Dean Kelly, in his classic *Why Conservative Churches Are Growing*, suggested that only when expectations were high and the call to discipline—discipleship—clearly spelled out, was there a resulting commitment. His suggestion to mainline, or liberal, churches was that they not receive new members too quickly. That advice has largely been ignored. No matter what sort of body one is discussing, as a rule when nothing is expected, nothing is produced. The best way to create inactive members is to assume that the evangelistic task is complete once their names have been added to the roll book.

Every Congregational Group an Educational Venture

While what I am about to suggest may seem like a dramatic departure in most places, we already have in place the primary tools to make it happen. Practically every manual on church growth recommends that new members be placed immediately in a face-to-face group. Studies indicate that converts or transfers who are not rooted in some programmatic or social body within the larger congregation tend to find the back door as quickly as they found the front door.

The change I am suggesting has to do with the nature of these smaller intracongregational units. Under the model we have been developing thus far, every group in the church needs to be a forum for reflection and action. They may not be called "classes." Indeed, learning would not be the only function. But they must be avenues through which growing Christians, as well as those who have been around for a long time, deal seriously with the meaning of the Christian faith.

First of all, the congregation needs to make a few fundamental decisions. As was the case at St. Paul's, vigorous remedial steps could not be taken to address the grave situation until the congregation realized that some radical retooling needed to be done. Coming to that awareness was essentially an educational issue. Also, if the body concludes that commitment lies at the heart of the problem and that commitment implies knowledge as well as motivation, then every group within the congregation can be redesigned.

Since most church groups are already part of the church's larger mission, the action part of the reflection-action continuum is set a priori. In most cases the revision is obvious. Let me cite some simple examples.

The choir's mission is to provide liturgical music. It sings the faith. Every rehearsal should begin with at least a fifteen-minute review of the meaning of the texts to be sung, including the hymns. If we are to vocalize our faith, what we sing needs to be an honest and reliable articulation of that faith, and those who proclaim the message ought to be aware of what they are proclaiming. Not only would the singers be better communicators of the gospel, but churches may be saved from so much of the religious pap currently called "Christian" music. This approach becomes problematic when churches select as choir leaders local musicians—public schoolteachers perhaps—who may have great musical gifts, but whose religious sensitivities are unknown, absent, or significantly out of harmony with the congregation's.

Every function or program unit in the congregation should spend a significant amount of the allotted meeting time reflecting on the way its particular task is related to the whole mission of the church. The why, the what, and the how become matters for serious discussion. In one useful parish model, all the committees meet on the same night of the month. If two hours are available, one hour is spent in study—led by the minister—and the second hour in committee work.

Obviously meetings of the teaching staff, including youth workers, should involve a careful look at the content as well as the context of teaching. And *nobody* should be turned loose as part of the congregation's teaching team prior to completing a disciplined course of study. And yet, even the best trained, most theologically alert teachers, who are usually with their children, youth, or adults less than an hour a week, cannot carry the educational burden of the church. It is, therefore, with some trepidation I suggest that the task must fall back on the home.

The Home as the Locus for Christian Education

There are five fundamental foci of learning for today's children: home, school, media, peers, and church. Clearly, the least effective is the last one on the list. Nobody in an hour or two a week can compete with twenty-five hours per week in school, and an estimated additional twenty-five before the TV set. The only one of the four nonchurch institutions we can otherwise appropriately access is the home. This means that the church must center its attention on equipping parents. To the extent many liberals have not taken seriously the evangelicals' interest in family values, we have missed our most significant educational opportunity. We may not mean, or even want to mean, everything our more conservative friends include in that term, but we fool ourselves if do not understand that whatever family constellation we are talking about, the basic theological task must be accomplished within such units.

I have come to the conclusion that the educational time and effort of church life for the foreseeable future must be expended on adults, particularly adult family members. While not forsaking the education of the children—we must beef up programs for them—we need to focus on their teachers, and in most cases that means parents. If we cannot get the attention of home-based adults, we will probably never get the attention of their children. In Babylon—in any Babylon—the stories must be told and the songs remembered where children eat, sleep, and are cuddled. While it may be important to have every child in the congregation in church school or some other in-house education program, it is far more important to have their parents, or other primary caregivers, in disciplined courses of study and action.

In recent years there has been an explosive increase in home schooling. While I believe all children need the socialization of the traditional public or private school, a significant number of parents have demonstrated that they can be more than adequate instructors in any of the basic academic areas. As a rule, when home-schooled children are later tested, they do as well as, or better than, those in the traditional public institutions. We cannot rely on either the public school or the usual parish program to provide the basic religious education of our children. The fundamental task must revert to the home, with the church supplementing and supporting what happens.

In addition to the in-church training of parents, it is essential that home-oriented curriculum materials be prepared. Not long ago I talked with the president of a major denominational publishing company. At one time these enterprises were lucrative. They did not *use* mission money; their sales *provided* resources to sustain other aspects of denominational life and work. These days church-owned presses are in serious financial trouble. I was told that the cash cow was formerly the marketing of church school curricula. That day is over. Denominational houses can redesign, rewrite, make more teacher-friendly, or almost give away new church school materials, but they will continue to sit, piled to the rafters in warehouses. It is both frustrating and useless to provide materials for church schools that no longer exist! What is needed are materials for home use, and supportive resources to help home-based adult teachers learn to use them.

What about the children who will not be part of homes where that is possible? I am less than sanguine about the universal appeal of what I am suggesting. Significant numbers of parents either can't or won't do what needs to be done. For those children, congregations need to act as a religious *in loco parentis*. In every congregation there are singles, childless couples, or grandparents who could take on a one-to-one assignment. Obviously those asked to assume this responsibility should be well equipped and carefully screened. And certainly the natural, adoptive, or foster parents should agree to the arrangement. Perhaps the best analogy may be found in the highly successful big sister, big brother, or foster grandparent programs of other organizations. It also might be possible to take groups of these youngsters and develop programs similar to the Cub Scouts. These small-group, intentional, home-based teaching and learning models combine both reflection and action. The possibilities for widening the Christian education of our children are limited only by our imaginations.

Intensive encounters such as youth retreats, summer camps and conferences, and even the district youth rally are times of potential spiritual stimulation and teaching. Many young people and children respond with great enthusiasm to these experiences, particularly with a closely knit group of old friends and new. Many lives—including mine—have been turned around in a week of camp or conference. Most children from church families find these experiences spiritually enriching and unforgettable. Even so, the close relationship between such programs and the home remains vital.

Beyond the Congregation

Powerful educational encounters can move out from the congregation and touch children who otherwise might never be in a church environment. Each year the congregation I served would find, through the juvenile court, twenty or thirty abused and neglected children and offer them a week at camp. Since the anonymity of these children usually from foster homes, needed to be preserved, special training had to take place for every staff person. Everything had to be done with the consent of the court, the foster parents, and, where possible, the biological or adoptive parents. While there were all the usual amenities of a good camp—swimming, horseback riding, crafts—the experience was rooted in a clearly defined religious ethos. Interactive Bible study took place for an hour and a half each morning. Services in the cabin groups and bedtime devotions were held daily. Camp songs were upbeat and consistent with the clear Christian theme of the week. This program, called The Royal Family Kids Camp, was adapted from a model developed by an Assembly of God congregation in California. Left-out children were told they were members of God's royal family. Most of the youngsters came to believe it, but not without doubts and the severe testing of everyone involved. After all, they had learned early in life that it is not safe to trust anyone.

With thirty youngsters we sent twenty adults to perform a variety of functions. The minister was the Bible teacher. Each "special friend" (counselor) had two children with whom she or he stayed around the clock. Each staff member was asked to attend a year-long series of preparatory sessions, which included hard theological work as well as camping nuts and bolts. In this action/reflection environment, amazing growth took place.

Staff members spent a week of vacation to work with these special children. Many others in the congregation were also involved in the mission. Supporting every staff member was a prayer partner, who stood with the staff at the dedicatory worship service and prayed for them and their children throughout the week. Supplies were gathered, a return meal and celebration planned, negotiations with public officials took place. In addition, each year the congregation put up several thousand dollars in new money to support the camp. That's the sort of dedication the mainline church must find if it is to emerge from its captivity with any power!

Who Will Do the Teaching?

If mainline congregations are to become communities of learners, who will do the teaching? When I graduated from seminary in the mid-1950s, I knew exactly how to deal with that problem. I would get a big enough church to have on the staff a full-time director of Christian education. Back then, seminaries had developed special programs for women who either were there to find a minister to marry or to become educational specialists. How times have changed—for the better! Women, often the ablest of the seminarians, are seldom interested in what was erroneously viewed as a subordinate position. Economics also took a hand. Except in a very limited number of large churches, there are no funds for a full-time education specialist. The great majority of modern congregations are fortunate to have the dollars to support one minister, and perhaps a part-time musician and a secretary.

Obviously, the day-to-day operation of the church's educational program must rest with the laity. Whether the church operates a traditional church school or engages in any of the other programs we have suggested, the operation must be in the hands of its members. Throughout this book I have resisted using the term "volunteer." Service in the church is not a voluntary activity. A volunteer can opt in and opt out, and is beholden to no one. To be a Christian implies a serious commitment; a vocation of service. There ought to be a distinct qualitative difference between the church and other community clubs and agencies that use the services of unremunerated workers.

As we have previously suggested, the minister must be the principal teacher. That means weekly meetings with the teaching staff. While the operation of the educational program is lay led, the content of that education is the province of the minister. Pastors can complain all day about the theological inadequacies of the typical church school staff. But whose task is it to see that everyone who touches the lives of these little ones is prepared? In the case of larger congregations, if the ministers cannot do all the teaching, they are responsible for training and monitoring those who do. Nevertheless, the main task falls on the ordained.

Among evangelicals with whom I have talked, it is almost inconceivable that sincere but untrained or spiritually inert layfolk would be turned loose on God's little ones. And it is the minister who sees to it that this never happens.

If, as we suggested in Chapter Four, the main task of the minister is to be the congregation's rabbi, it is vital that he or she be responsible for the theological education of not only new members and the front-line education staff, but also other members of the parish. For many years I have taken personal responsibility for teaching a church school class of younger adults, most of whom are new to the church. In addition, one afternoon and often one evening a week have been spent in serious study with other church members, and even those beyond the congregation. I have never talked down or protected these students from dealing with serious and profound biblical and theological issues. Sessions have been recorded, on tape and on film, because those who missed a class were expected to review it later. Notes were taken and reading required. What I discovered in my own education and subsequent scholarly pursuits was shared with members of these classes.

Once I came to the conclusion that my primary task was to be the theologian in residence, my priorities, my schedule, and my personal discipline dramatically changed. The work of the congregation was turned back to the laity, to whom it properly belonged. I was consumed in study, preparation for sermons and lectures, a variety of other teaching functions, and tutoring those with special needs and questions. Most of the remainder of my hours were spent being a pastor. For a time, some aspects of the life of the church suffered. The minister was not doing much administration, marketing, programming, or planning. Once members of the congregation realized that these things belonged in their portfolios, not mine, things picked up. The Old Testament scholar, Walter Brueggemann, has suggested that justice implies finding out what belongs to whom, and returning it to them. In our era, the program and life of the church belong to the laity. The theological task and the equipping of the saints for their work of ministry belongs to the theologian in residence. It is by that division of labor that congregations can once more become communities of learning.

Questions for Reflection and Discussion

1. Review the history of Christian education in your congregation. Is the Sunday church school as vital and well attended as it used to be? What percentage of your grade school and high school students are regular attendees? Is it easy to recruit teachers, and how are they prepared for their classroom assignments? Do you expect that your teachers have some substantial background before they are turned loose on a group of children?

2. Are you familiar with the curriculum materials currently being used in the church school classes in your congregation? Are they theologically solid, or were they chosen simply because they are easy to teach?

3. If your church school is not in vigorous health, what other educational opportunities does your congregation provide?

4. Does your minister (always—often—occasionally—never) use his or her sermon time as a teaching opportunity? Many sermons these days focus on entertainment. Preachers like to hear folks say they enjoyed the sermon. How can a solid teaching sermon also be enjoyable?

5. If the author is correct, and the future of mainline religion is dismal without a renewal of commitment on the part of church members, evaluate the level of commitment in your congregation. In what ways might Christian education be at the heart of a search for a more committed church constituency?

6. What do the members of the church really expect of each other, or are expectations and standards rarely mentioned for fear of offending somebody? What standards of faithfulness, work, stewardship, and service are new members of the congregation expected to maintain?

7. List all the face-to face groups in the congregation. How many of them include a learning/action component in their work? Who does the teaching? In what specific ways is what is learned given theological substance? If not, how might the church program be altered so that everybody becomes a learner in at least one context?

8. Does your congregation provide any materials, training, or encouragement so that the home becomes a primary locus of Christian education? What resources would you like to see developed to make this happen?

9. Evaluate the leadership role of your minister in the educational life of the congregation. How could she/he be freed up to become a more effective "theologian in residence"?

7 Spiritual Formation and the Worshiping Community

It has been said that a certain very liberal Christian group is made up of people who have long since given up on religion, but cannot break the habit of going to church. I often wonder if many of us in mainline congregations have rejected almost anything that smacks of the holy, the mystical, or the charismatic. If *they* do it, it must be wrong! On the other hand, there is a growing conversation in the liberal community about spiritual formation. The architect of liberation theology, Gustavo Gutierrez, decided a decade ago that any action not rooted in spirituality was outside the Christian tradition. Every subsequent book he has written, beginning with *We Dig from Our Own Wells*, has been about Christian spirituality.

The Quest for Spirituality

In mainline and ecumenical seminaries there has been a steady reemphasis on spiritual formation, the power of prayer, identification with God, and the contemplative life. In many cases these emphases have not been attempts to flee from the world, but to engage it at its deepest level. Process theology is not other-worldly or enamored with the supernatural or mystical experience. But neither does it leave God somewhere in the skies, omnipotent and remote. In process thought, God is intimately involved with all of human life, and the life of the Christian is profoundly interwoven with the purpose, will, and mind of God. What each does affects the other.

It is this relationship that may provide the mainline church with the clearest entrée to spiritual formation. The God of our faith is not some aloof person who can be manipulated by prayer or another pious activity into doing what we want done. Rather, God is in our midst as fellow sojourner, partner, intimate author of goodness, love, and creativity. It is this God who suffers for us and with us, who is touched by our infirmities, and who shares our pain and takes it on as God's own. Thus the heart of Christian process theology is the cross. God is affected by our sin. We are reconciled by God's gracious action in Christ.

As much as we are committed to the findings of science and the insights of the rational, empirical, and scholarly world, we must never be reduced to a flat scientism ruled only by what is referred to as the "law of nature." We hold that the greatest unexplored world in the universe is the inner world of the Spirit, and we seek to be caught up in that world—which is none other than this world! And yet God is not a pal or a buddy or even good friends, but that Mystery

> Uncomprehended and unbought,
> Beyond all knowledge and all thought.

If the contemporary mainline church has been long on marketing, program development, community spirit, and being "with it," it has been painfully short on helping people to develop deeper, more profound relationships with God. It is almost as if we are afraid that if we do anything that smacks of the overwhelming sense of the presence of the Holy Spirit, we will become just like "them."

The Larger Spirituality

David Tacey, in his book *Edge of the Sacred*, writes about the loss of spirituality in Australia, one of the Western world's most secular societies. He quotes Jung, who held, "The Intellectual Enlightenment, which drained the world of its psychic and spiritual content, and located the psyche only within the human being, was an important step in the history of consciousness. It was the stage in which religion was replaced by humanism, and in which myth and magic were gradually dislodged by the sciences" (154). As powerful and important as the scientific revolution has been, the loss of spirituality is death-dealing to the soul, which will do almost anything in an effort to fill the vacuum. We cannot live alone in this universe. The sense of isolation and terror, the great existential *angst*, is overwhelming. We are part of a larger system, that of the Spirit, which religions we call "primitive" never lost.

A profound spirituality affirms that the universe is interactive. That is, everything affects everything else. What happens anywhere affects what is real everywhere. The flutter of a parrot's feather in Fiji may ultimately result in a hurricane that hits the Florida coast. Herein lies one of the amazing spiritual discoveries of quantum mechanics. One cannot even measure a natural phenomenon without the measurer, and the instrument by which the measurement is done, altering the outcome. The Gaia, the animating principle of the universe, is affected by the thought of the most remote aboriginal, just as the earth around that "primitive" is in an interactive relationship to every person.

In the Christian tradition we observe and stand in dynamic relationship to this power and authority in Jesus, who was "incarnate of the Holy Spirit, and became man." The incarnation takes the material world, the Gaia, seriously. There is a living cosmos with which we stand in living relationship. We testify to the spirituality of the universe with a birth announced to shepherds, then water, bread and wine, and finally an event on a hillside outside Jerusalem's city walls.

Christian thought that has attempted to limit spirituality to the non-earthly or non-physical has robbed us of the richest part of our world. As Tacey put it, "It is a great tragedy that the human psyche could only be discovered by first destroying or denying the spiritual essence of the greater world, as if we in the West were so attached to the world that we had to kill it off before we could come to ourselves" (154).

We do not tend to think of ecology, for instance, as particularly related to spirituality. But the ecological movement is profoundly spiritual, far beyond the romantic notion that we are the saviors of the world if we recycle our plastics. There is more at stake than our capacity to stir up collective guilt because of what we have done to

Spiritual Formation and the Worshiping Community 95

the air and the rivers. The ecological crisis is at bottom a spiritual crisis. The environment is not something out there, as if we were detached from it. Nor is God something or someone out there who exists independently of everything else. An organic—spiritual—relationship exists among God, the natural world, and the human consciousness. The secular and purely moral approach to this problem simply will not work, because the issues are deeper than most activists' programs will allow. The true ecological task is not only to repair the damage we have caused to the outer world, but to repair the deep splits on the inside; to work toward inclusive, rather than exclusive, concepts of selfhood and identity. It is the whole world that is to be redeemed, which stands on tiptoes, eager to see the children of God coming into their own (Tacey 151f.).

Tacey is deeply critical of organized religion, and calls into question a notion of theology limited to ideology or words about God.

> If Christianity survives the outbreak of the spirit, it will be only that the times have changed, and that a new style of religious life is demanded. The living spirit is not particularly concerned with belief or dogma, but is more concerned with experience and transformation. Already congregations are warming to ministers and priests who emphasize the experience of spirit rather than belief in the statements of scripture. Churches that invite or encourage an inward experience of spirit are at least holding their own. However, the positive changes within the official structures cannot keep up with the demands, and this is one reason why spiritualistic churches, charismatic born-again groups and revivalists movements, are gaining enormous followings (126).

Taking Tacey's main arguments, we can affirm that if by theology we mean only doctrine, we are in a captivity of our own making from which we may never recover. But theology cannot be divorced from experience. In personal terms that means a deeper exploration of the inner journey. In terms of community it means intense interaction within the community of faith. In terms of others it means social action. In terms of the natural world it means the transformation of the human consciousness so that we recognize our oneness with that world. In terms of God it means a celebration of the one who is present, the "I Am" in our midst, related both to nature and to history. It is this God with us and among us with whom we make the inward journey.

At this point, however, I must offer an important caveat. There is a danger that in our hunger for the spiritual, the experiential, the mystical, we look in the wrong direction or act impulsively out of lonely desperation. We may think that some political program or human relationship will supply it. Drug and alcohol addiction, all forms of sexual expression, new highs that satisfy only temporarily and call for even higher highs are attempted. We fly in tiny airplanes, and when that no longer provides the anticipated buzz, we jump out of them. When that thrill gives out, we leap from cliffs with homebuilt wings, or fling ourselves off bridges with rubber bands wrapped around our ankles. But no matter how high the high we achieve, it fails to fill the profound inner vacant places for very long.

Every hot musical group must be louder and more violent than that last. The ultimate word about experience is that nothing is ever enough—there is always the next level. It is like a drug that must be taken in larger and larger doses to achieve the same palliative effect. Experiential religion, to remain popular, has got to reach for ever higher emotional highs. In my community each new successful charismatic church has had to outdo its older brothers and sisters in reaching for more exotic forms of expression. In many places we are now at a point where the most popular churches find the faithful falling to the floor in uncontrolled fits of laughter. No telling what might come next. And the world crying out to be redeemed cries alone.

Secularity is itself an effort to fill a void with things, places, goods, objects, clothes, cosmetics, big luxury items, summer cottages, or whatever takes us beyond the mundane and ordinary. Happiness is that temporary feeling that comes when the amount of the economic drug is increased or its potency heightened. We seek a nirvana with what money can buy; but no matter how much we invest, it never is enough to provide a down payment on a ticket to that land. The more, bigger, and louder do little other than provide a temporary palliative to silence the cry of pain that comes up from the void we have created with the death of God. We are forced to turn to an orgy—religious and otherwise—for relief. We overburden the physical by asking it to perform magical tricks and to produce miraculous satisfactions. And it all turns demonic. Satan is, after all, a fallen angel, a distortion and parody of the sacred, an effort to produce godliness by forsaking God.

The heart of religion is that deep which calls to deep; the inner voice which must cry out "Holy! Holy! Holy!" lest it die. This quest for intimacy is the heart of not only process thought, but of all authentic Christian theology. But for many mainliners all this may seem like too much religion. We are leery of being "born of the spirit, washed in the blood." The story and song we have tend to be flat and pedestrian.

If the mainline church is to make it through these years of captivity, and emerge with a story worth telling and the power to tell it, we must rediscover the power of spirituality. Without it there is not much our children will find worth learning, and their drift into the religion of secularism will be complete.

Spirituality and Public Worship

Nowhere is the dilemma more apparent than in our current quandary about public worship. Obviously there is more than one way or formula for the conduct of public worship. Both the stately and profoundly moving high-church drama and the informal rhythmic dynamism of the African celebratory rite can be Christian worship.

Old formulas and new music can be equally authentic. Nevertheless, there are some disturbing clues as to how lost and bewildered the mainline church seems to be. The question is this: How do we maintain liturgical integrity and at the same time endow worship with vigor, experiential and emotional power, and contemporary style? I will not burden you with things I once attempted, all the way from tying up groups with a rope to make some point that now seems to escape me, to having someone pop—born again—out of a large plastic sack. I have employed jazz bands, a multimedia show with seventeen projectors going at the same time, and even guerrilla theater with both God and the devil speaking over offstage loudspeakers. You name it and I've tried it. While these gimmicks drew crowds and generated the best free show in town, I'm not certain they constituted Christian worship.

In the past year I have worshiped in a variety of mainline churches. While I never failed to be pointed toward God in any of the services, only occasionally did I come away warmed and filled, or having a sense that I was in the presence of the Holy. Some churches were simply deadly dull. If someone were to go home and be asked what happened, the accurate answer would have been, "Many things were said, but nothing seemed to happen." I have been in cavernous buildings that held a handful of people who didn't sing the hymns, follow the reading of the texts, say the printed prayers, or seem moved at any point by anything. In some churches the music and the words could have been replicated from a service held a hundred years ago. Nothing wrong with that. What *was* wrong was that if at one time there had been a sense of the presence of God or deep calling to deep, it was now a distant memory. Wesley talked about hearts strangely warmed. Too often I felt I was in an assembly of those whose hearts had been decently chilled.

Other congregations were trying harder to move from boredom to new life. The temptation seems to have been to mimic evangelical churches, which in turn mimic the entertainment-centered TV religionists. Chancels have been transformed into sound stages. Everything is done for the pleasing effect it might have on the audience. Musicians run from pipe organ to piano to electronic keyboard in an attempt to produce the right mood, which must be adjusted every few minutes lest boredom set in. And when did we get the idea that everything should be met with applause? Worship might be entertaining—in a sense—but it is not entertainment.

Worship is that corporate act in which people are pointed to God, drawn to God, opened to God. Symbolically, it is the God above and the God within and among. The initiative is God's. The response is ours. And that response is centered in thanksgiving. Increasingly in Protestant churches that formerly celebrated the Lord's Supper—the Eucharist—only monthly or quarterly, there is growing interest in making the feast of thanksgiving not merely part of daily or weekly worship, but rather the reason worship services are held. The newly designed liturgy, produced by the Consultation on Church Union, is primarily a communion service, which may include preaching.

Even though it makes most mainliners uneasy, we are seeing an increased effort to bring physical bodies into liturgical activities. Caution still prevails. If there is dance, it will be by a performing group.

Most of us are not ready to get up and dance in the aisles. The charismatic practice of "lifting holy hands to God," or swaying in prayer, is frightening to many of us. Yet, I have always been moved when I have had the opportunity to preach to African-American congregations. You know somebody is out there, not just in a remote spiritual sense, but bodily! Spirituality involves the whole of existence, and that includes the physical. Christian art, music, architecture testify to an incarnate, bodied faith.

While churches with traditional liturgies always included more than one brief biblical text, now among many free churches the Scriptures, the wellspring of spirituality, are being more widely read. Readings from the Bible are not just devices to provide the preacher with a text.

We are also seeing the production of a plethora of new denominational hymnals, which include gospel choruses, old standards, and solid new poetry. I trust we have gotten past the liturgical snobbishness that insisted if a tune was singable by a congregation it wasn't worth singing. At the same time, we have attempted to see that the texts have more theological integrity. Images of God rooted in a Greek philosophic world are still with us, but we are not taking them quite as literally as we once did. Gone, or going, are gender exclusive poems, or those that deify dominion and conquest. If in our age there is an abundance of political correctness, there is also a growing sensitivity to the relationship between the authentic articulation of the faith and the way in which we provide artistic symbolization.

In many mainline congregations these days there tends to be more lay participation and less distancing of the people from the "real" action. Two generations ago we were falling all over ourselves in an effort to capture what our Roman Catholic brothers and sisters had found historically valid. Almost every Protestant church building that was constructed or remodeled divided the chancel and put the communion table as far from the people as possible. About the same time, Catholics moved the altar away from the wall and made it a holy table on or near the level of the congregation. Now Protestants find themselves remodeling again.

If there is a hunger for the proper, there is a deeper hunger for the spiritual, and while dullness may too often still be the operative—or inoperative—word, the waters are moving.

As for waters, efforts are also being made to recapture the profoundly spiritual nature of baptism. It is not a pretty ceremony in which parents have a coming-out party for their newborns. It is the testimony that God claims each of us at birth and grafts us into a family of faith. The power of the holy waters is even more evident when baptism is the act by which new believers give physical utterance to the faith they have just proclaimed.

No adventurer begins a journey into the unknown with photographic certainty where the road will lead or what will be encountered en route. Earlier in this century Halford Luckock preached a sermon I could mentally reproduce to this day. It was entitled "Marching off the Map." It described Abram's journey to a land he was to receive as an inheritance—"By faith...Abraham went out, not knowing where he was to go." There is a hunger abroad in our day for more religious certainty. People will throw themselves into almost anything in order to find the security Mark Twain described as "the calm confidence of a Christian with four aces." Spirituality, however, may imply quite the opposite. While those in Babylonian captivity need verities in which to root their hope, they must prepare the generation that will return to Jerusalem with the will and the spirit to adventure into the unknown—to march off the known maps.

Wherever worship is headed, we will not find the right paths by making surveys of what people want, trivializing the rite by becoming entertainers, holding focus groups, or determining what sells. Authentic spirituality is subject to the winds of God, which blow through us and which fill us—baptize us—as the *Spirit* wills, not where we predict or suggest it should.

No matter how it comes to be structured, worship in the mainline church must share the following characteristics.

- It will endeavor to develop a deeper relationship between God and the assembled congregation.
- It will be corporate, not simply private devotions being performed by a number of individuals who happen to be in the same place.
- While paying respect and giving attention to the historic faith of the church, it will seek to employ images and notions drawn from the life of the people in both its sacred and its secular manifesta-

tions. At the same time it will be honest about scholarship and the impact of a contemporary world.
- It will command the attention and interest of the worshipers, and will involve their bodies, as well as their minds.
- It will be of, for, and by the people, not a performance put on for their amusement.
- It will be a celebration of the mighty acts of God.
- It will hear and respond to the witness of the people of God as evidenced in both scripture and tradition.
- Its language and the way theology is artistically symbolized will speak in terms that are inclusive and gracious.
- It will be a service of both word and sacrament.

The Ministry of Healing

Thus far we have been speaking of the main Sunday morning service of the congregation. While public worship is possible any time during the week, Sunday morning will probably remain the generally observed time for the foreseeable future. Mainline congregations that have attempted to hold services on Thursday night, to capture a group that has other things to do on Sundays, have reported that people who will find reasons not to worship on Sunday morning will not turn out in substantial numbers on Thursday evening. There may, however, be a variety of different sorts of services held for smaller groups within the congregation that will take place at other times.

Since in this chapter we are particularly concerned about spirituality, we now turn our attention to an evidence of spiritual vitality that has been not only largely ignored by the mainline church, but treated with considerable suspicion. I refer to services focused on healing.

Often when religious people use the word "save," they automatically attach the word "soul." The two words, however, are unconnected. The biblical tradition is not so much concerned with saving souls as it is with offering wholeness. To save is to restore, reconcile, make whole or well a physical body, spirit, or relationship. It is to repair that which is broken. In the mythological story of Eden, our first parents were forced to leave Eden and live in an unreconciled and broken world. The alienation was fourfold. They were separated from self, from one another, from nature, and from God. The rest of the Bible is the story of how God has been at work to overcome the separation and mend the brokenness. If to be saved is to be healed, when the word "heal" is used in a religious context we tend to equate it with "cured." While the biblical tradition is replete with stories of physical healing, the making whole of broken bodies is only one aspect of the reconciliation God has been at work to bring about. There are not only broken bodies, there are broken hearts, broken relationships, broken spirits. The notion of original sin may be, at center, a testimony that life comes to us broken. And apart from God's love and care that is how most people experience it day after day.

The healing ministry of Jesus dealt with all four of the broken areas of human existence. While we usually think of physical healings, a careful reading of the Gospels indicates miraculous cures to be only one part of a larger concern. And yet, one cannot read the Gospels faithfully without sensing Jesus' profound concern for those with broken bodies. The book of Acts testifies that this emphasis was present in the church from the beginning. Later, hospitals were established by Christians who knew that physical as well as spiritual suffering must be subject to the compassion of Christ's body.

Love, in the Christian context, has always been understood in relationship. God does not love us in the abstract but in flesh and blood. The Christian faith is not, and never has been, concerned about saving souls, or showing people how to escape from this world and enter a better one up there somewhere. At the same time, our faith has always understood that there is a tension between body and spirit. A few years back, during the heyday of humanistic psychology, we were fond of saying, "We don't have bodies; we are bodies." That may be the truth, but it is not the whole truth. Neither do the physical sciences tell us all about life we need to know. While we must rely on science, and celebrate its enormous power for good, we cannot turn over to secularists the task of making whole that which is broken. Perhaps the mainline church has been too quick to abandon a concern for the healing of the body in ways other than the use of secular medicine.

Other Christians have stepped into the hiatus we have created. If, on the one hand, we have turned over the therapeutic enterprise to secular science, on the other hand we have allowed charlatans to carry on much of the religious aspect of the healing arts. But having left the field, we have little right to criticize those who have seen the need. There is a relationship between faith and wholeness, and despite the tricks they might play and the manipulation in which they engage, the Oral Roberts and the Benny Hinns of the religious world give more than a nod to the power of the Spirit. Every congregation, therefore, needs to look again at the relationship between spirituality and healing—or salvation.

Shortly after Pentecost, Peter and John encountered a beggar as they were walking near the temple. You remember Peter's response to the plea for alms. "I have no silver or gold, but what I have I give you; in the name of Jesus Christ of Nazareth, stand up and walk" (Acts 3:6). Today we can sidestep the power of the text by explaining that we have silver and gold, and that we use it supporting medical technology. But as a spiritual discipline, we no longer seem able to say, "Rise and walk."

Physicians tell us that the great majority of patients who enter their examination rooms are suffering from troubles that have their roots in spiritual distress. While never claiming to produce cures that violate the laws of nature, we cannot abandon the spiritual energy and support that leads to reconciliation, wholeness, and health. Beyond physical illness, there are many other forms of brokenness. Every time I have looked out over a congregation, I knew I was in the midst of people with broken hearts, broken lives, broken relationships, broken spirits, broken promises, and broken minds. It is not that we have nothing to *say*, but it is rare that we have anything we are able to *do*.

For many years the congregation I last served held regular services to which the broken were invited. Here was an action/reflection model in which we *spoke* about the power of the gospel and then *did* something. We gathered around the broken as they knelt in our midst. We placed our hands on their heads and prayed for them. And wholeness often came. Sometimes people with physical troubles would get well. Sometimes broken relationships would be mended. Sometimes grief would be relieved and people could get back to living again.

Sometimes wholeness meant allowing a person to die, or giving them the strength to die graciously in the arms of God and their friends. We never told God ahead of time what we expected to be done. God, who is already deeply and profoundly involved with us moment by moment, was in our midst, weeping as we wept, and rejoicing as we rejoiced. At the very least, those who knelt in the midst of this company of believers knew they were profoundly loved. And, after all, isn't that the root of the gospel and of spiritual power?

The worshiping group was called the Ebb Tide Fellowship. It was composed of those whose lives were at ebb tide, for whom the waters of hope had vanished. With them were other Christians who wanted to share their burdens. Described in the following pages is enough of the service to give you the flow and texture of what we did. You will not see reproduced, however, the spiritual energy, commitment, and focus that filled the room each time we gathered.

AN ORDER OF SERVICE FOR THE EBB TIDE FELLOWSHIP

THE OPENING PRAYER

Leader: Gracious God, we thank you for your mercies that are new every day; for health and strength, for this day with its opportunities for work, and joy, and service. We pray for your help as we face the duties to be done, the temptations that confront us, and the disappointments that may await us. Hold us in your arms, even as we hold each other in the arms of faith and prayer. AMEN.

(There follows a thankful litany in which we remember the goodness of God as seen in our history and in our lives.)

A PRAYER FOR PEACE (adopted from a prayer of St. Francis of Assisi)

All: Lord, make us instruments of your peace.
  Where there is hatred, let us sow love;
  Where there is injury, pardon;
  Where there is doubt, faith;
  Where there is despair, hope;
  Where there is darkness, light;
  Where there is sadness, joy.
  O Divine Master, grant that we may not so much seek to be consoled as to console; to be understood, as to understand; to be

loved, as to love; for it is in giving that we receive; it is in pardoning that we are pardoned; it is in dying that we are born to eternal life.

WE ACKNOWLEDGE OUR BROKENNESS AND OUR SINS

(There follows an adaptation of one of the traditional confessions of sin, or one in modern language written for the occasion. For broken people, who know all too well the extent of their alienation, it does little good to say, "And there is no health in us." Instead, there would be words such as, "and sometimes it seems as if there is no health in us." Periods of silence and reflection were interspersed throughout the litany. As in every confession of sin, there follows an assurance of forgiveness.)

FROM THE TESTIMONY OF THE PEOPLE OF GOD (It had become the practice in the congregation to respond to readings from the Scriptures with: "This is a testimony of the people of God.")

(There follows a thirty-minute study of a biblical passage, using a dialogic form of probing the text, developed by Walter Wink. Texts were often memorized, spontaneously dramatized by those present, probed for new meanings, examined critically, and applied to the lives of those present. This part of the service concludes with the following prayer offered by the leader.)

Leader: Almighty God, who governs all things in heaven and on earth, mercifully hear all our prayers, and grant to us in this community of faith, and others for whom we pray, all things that they need. Strengthen the faithful; visit and relieve the sick; bless and protect the children; turn and soften the wicked; arouse the careless; restore the fallen; rescue the penitent; remove all hindrances to the advancement of your truth; and bring us all to be of one heart and mind, to the glory of your Holy Name. AMEN.

A CALL TO PRAYER FOR OTHERS

Leader: Our Lord Christ has said, "Come to me all who labor and are heavy laden, and I will give you rest." And so now we come before God, asking for healing for ourselves, and for all kinds of people, known and unknown to us. We pray for the wholeness that God gives. May the Spirit be present in our lives, that we may perform the vocation God has given each of us, as we seek to serve our sisters and brothers.

(There follows a series of prayers in which we name specific persons, places, and conditions.)

We remember those who are hospitalized or who are recovering from illness, especially…

We remember those in trouble, especially…

We remember those in places where there is turmoil, unrest, war, and bitterness, especially…

We pray for the healing of God's people, for peace and unity in the church, and for our Christian friends in other communions, especially…

We pray for those who have died, and whose faith we remember, and those whose faith is known to you alone; that with all the saints they have rest where there is no pain or grief anymore, especially…

(We then prepare to pray for those who are in our midst.)

All: O living Christ, make us conscious of your presence. Touch our eyes that we may see you. Open our ears that we may hear you. Enter our hearts that we may love you. And make us whole even as we pray for others.

(At this point the leader invites to the front of the chapel, one at a time, those who desire the prayers of the fellowship. Sometimes there were a dozen, sometimes one or two, and sometimes no one. Often the leader would say a word about the specific problem. It was the rule of the fellowship that nothing was ever mentioned beyond the room. To my knowledge that pledge was never violated, nor was the prayer service advertised except by word of mouth and notice in the church's newsletter. People who came to the front knelt if they were able, and received the hands of as many as could gather around them. The leader, or some other person, would offer prayer for them. They would rise to receive the tears and the embraces of many who were present.)

A TIME FOR THANKSGIVING

(There follows the joyful testimonies of those ready to offer thanksgiving for healing, for some new insight, for some broken place made whole, or for any other reconciling experience.)

THE BLESSING AND BENEDICTION
Leader: The grace of God be in our eyes,
People: That we may proclaim God's gladness.
(There follows a litany of thanksgiving, ending with the words):
Leader: Let us go forth in the name of Christ!
People: Thanks be to God!
Leader: The peace of the Lord be with you always!
People: And with you!

As the service of the Ebb Tide Fellowship concludes we greet one another, sharing the joy of the risen Christ, who is alive in our hearts and lives.

"Centering," and the Dilemma of Personal Devotions

While most members of mainline churches put prayer and Bible study high on their list of religious "shoulds," these personal devotional acts are often admired from a distance. While there are exhortations, available resources, and much conversation, our churches are not consistently immersed in these disciplines. The reasons often have to do with a fuzzy theology. Many modern people find it difficult to believe in, let alone converse with, the traditional notion of God as a supernatural being, who lives somewhere in the sky and who looks down with love and judgment on those below. Somehow the exercise in bowing the head, closing the eyes, and shifting into an archaic form of English no longer seems real. Lacking a disciplined prayer life we are haunted by guilt. Perhaps prayer will become possible for many in the discovery that God is present, involved, shaped by what we do and fail to do, even as our lives are shaped by the divine presence.

There is a wordless spirituality in which one sits quietly and waits for the leading of the Spirit. Most mainliners have much to learn from the Quakers, whose worship and whose lives tend to be deeply spiritual. But it is a quiet spirituality in which there is little speaking or attempts to form words and ideas, but rather relies on an openness to the power of the gathered community and the sanctity of stillness. Like clay on a potter's wheel, Quakers have learned the art of centering their lives until the spinning clay appears to be motionless—a still point in a turning world. It is then that the potter can open the clay and make a useful vessel. Instead of beginning meetings, classes, and services with traditional prayer, perhaps a congregation that learns the skill of centering can set a richer tone for what follows. Thus in the context of *doing* spirituality, those present can come to a new awareness of what it is to practice the presence of God.

The Spirit and Spirituality

If mainline churches have often focused their attention on the fruits of the Spirit (love, joy, peace, patience, kindness, generosity, gentleness, faithfulness, self-control), we have not always known what to make of the gifts of the Spirit, or the baptism in the Spirit. We are cautious about such things as speaking in tongues: indeed, we tend to be hostile. Our religion is rational. The excesses of the charismatics do little for us.

I recently attended the morning worship service of a freewheeling independent congregation of about two thousand members. It began with forty-five minutes worth of "praise songs," in which simple lyrics, displayed on large screens, were repeated over and over again, with increasing intensity. It was essentially a rock concert with all the emotion, dancing, shouting, hand waving, and hype necessary to get the crowd in the right mood. In addition to taking the offering and a ten-minute "roast" by way of introducing the soloist, there was much lighthearted banter between the warm-up act—the chief musician—and the pastor. The remainder of the service consisted of a fifty-minute sermon and a fifteen-minute altar call. While speaking, or shouting, in tongues was everywhere evident, there was no effort by anyone to interpret what was purportedly being uttered by the Spirit.

It is this sort of manipulative emotional excess that drives many mainline Christians to the other end of the spectrum. If that is what it means to be baptized in the Spirit or to exercise spiritual gifts, we don't want any part of it. The religion of many of our more thoughtful church members often moves no lower than the cerebral cortex. There may not be any emotional excess, but neither is there much joy or dancing before the Lord, or finding the love and mercy of God so overpowering that normal words cannot contain the feeling. And thus there is little awe and not much sense of being in the presence of the Holy. Few seraphim fly from smoking altars with hot coals, and few lips seem touched.

Spiritual Formation and the Worshiping Community

Not everyone, however, is moved by the same stimuli, nor do we universally show or feel emotions in the same way. I am deeply moved by traditional hymns, the communion of the Lord's Supper, the warmth of the assembled congregation. A service I might find dull, others may experience as drawing from deep wells.

Whatever else the mainline church does during its Babylonian captivity, it needs to recover a sense of *passion*. Passion, not excitement, is the operative principle. There are bodies that advertise themselves as "The Most Exciting Church in Town." But excitement has become an end in itself. There may be a passion to make others as they are, and to call that activity "being saved," but there is little inclusive love, commitment to the poor, the left out, and those quite unlike themselves.

Methodism was born partly out of the sense that emotional sterility was not to be equated with the gospel, and that a faith that did not touch the heart was not a faith worth having. When throughout church history there have been emotionally charged revivals or awakenings, they have most often been attempts to recover the passion of the gospel.

It may be that we have entered another such period, and the charismatic movement is a testimony that spiritual awareness and power abhors the vacuum created by a Protestantism that is so intellectually proper it never gets from the head to the heart. Neither the public worship of God nor the private devotions of the Christian can be reduced to a scholarly exercise. If we have learned how to love God with all our minds, we are yet far short of heeding what Jesus called the greatest commandment if we have not yet learned to love God with all our hearts. The sort of commitment for which we long and which we must engender if we are to survive these years of drought will not come if we are devoid of a religion that weeps, dances, heals, and loves aloud.

Questions for Reflection and Discussion

1. When you think of spirituality do your images go beyond prayer, meditation, and the other quiet interior disciplines? If so, what else might you include?

2. The ancient Persians believed there were two separate worlds: the world of the spirit and the physical world. In what way do many modern Christians still make this distinction? What difference does it make whether we think of (a) a living God among us who continually seeks us out, or (b) a God out there who is pure spirit and whom we must continually seek out in prayer and meditation?

3. Modern science has affirmed that everything in the universe is related to everything else. How does this notion make a difference in how we understand God's relationship to the world—and thus to spirituality?

4. For Christians the incarnation—God coming among us in Jesus—lies at the heart of our faith. Does this make a difference in how we are encountered by the divine in our daily lives? What are the implications for the way we treat the natural world?

5. On page 95 the author spells out how a broader and more penetrating notion of spirituality affects the following: the individual, the community of faith, the wider society, and the natural world. What do you sense are the implications for the work of the church in each of these areas?

6. Think about the worship services of your congregation. Are they spiritually rich? What does that phrase mean? Are worship services put on for their entertainment value? Are there ways that both ancient and modern symbols are used? Try to state the purpose and thrust of public worship in a single sentence.

7. If the body is a vehicle for the spirit, in what ways does your weekly worship service involve the five senses? Or is spirituality reduced to sitting quietly?

8. In what ways do the sacraments of baptism and the Eucharist employ the physical? Insofar as they do, does this make them less spiritual?

9. Does your church have a healing ministry? How does it function in the whole life of the church? What do you think of the "Ebb Tide Service" described beginning on page 104?

8 | Evangelism and Social Witness

In both congregational and denominational structures, evangelism and social witness have traditionally been viewed as separate and distinct. Personal salvation and the social gospel were not to be confused. Evangelism dealt with how people are brought to faith in Christ. Social witness was how the church acts on behalf of the neglected, the poor, and the downtrodden; or ways in which the church speaks to political, economic, and other issues in secular culture. In most congregations two very different committees handled these functions, and generally two very different types of members served on them. Often conflicts within the congregation focused around these differences. The evangelists came to believe that the social activists were wrong in their opinions; and besides that, they kept folks who didn't care for all that political talk out of the church. The activists came to believe that the evangelists were interested only in saving souls, and couldn't care less about the real problems facing real people.

The same issue, on a larger scale, confronted denominations. As funds for denominational work slowly withered, the conflict took on serious economic implications. Money was just not available to do everything. New priorities had to be established. Something had to give. Common sense seemed to suggest that if somebody's budget had to be dealt a body blow, it had better be those least able to develop new financial resources. Often at the top of the list of non-performers were departments of social witness. Since the future of the church required the recruitment of significant numbers of new members, it was widely held that those who pushed social concerns not only failed to increase budgets, but also had a deleterious effect on giving at every level. It was assumed that people were leaving mainline churches in droves, driven away by liberal programs and pronouncements emanating from denominational headquarters out of touch with what the people in the pews were thinking. Of particular significance was the support of feminists, gays, and lesbians, and those concerned about abortion rights. An interdenominational conference held in 1993 concerned with "Re-Imaging" the role of women in the church and in society, sparked vigorous protests. It was widely believed that one could chart the loss of revenues with each new so-called radical episode, assembly resolution, or controversial issue debated.

In most mainline denominations there arose small but increasingly powerful contingents of conservatives, who spent almost full-time beating on what they saw as the liberal gates of the church's bureaucracy. Even though these conservative groups constituted only a tiny minority of the memberships of most mainline denominations, they exercised enormous clout. In denomination after denomination funds and staff were cut from the social witness departments and their programs. Mainline churches were already facing a dim future, and fighting one more losing battle was more than most church executives were willing to tackle.

The obvious answer to the grave issues facing mainline churches was to move away from social action and toward evangelism. Since there were no direct ways in which denominations could engage in evangelism, the weight of the problem was thrust back on congregations. Empowering and sustaining congregations as vital faith communities became the rallying cry in communion after communion. It was the local congregation that was at the root of the trouble, and therefore every effort needed to be expended to beef up these community-based units. What is more, they were closest to the people; and since the church was rather like a democracy, ecclesiastical officials needed to pay attention to what they were saying. For a variety of distressing reasons, folks in the pews tended to be far more conservative than those in denominational offices.

Local structures were to be retooled in order to place evangelism at the top of the agenda. That was the message almost universally heard. Congregations had to be moved away from social action, and returned to what they really knew was the essence of their mission—"winning people to Christ." This articulated strategy, emanating from denominational headquarters, came as good news down in the pews, where social witness was increasingly unpopular.

The implementation of the strategy, however, seemed to make no serious impact on the problem. Congregations continued to lose strength, and year after year denominational statistics continued to plummet. Social action did not prove to be the culprit. People left whether or not congregations were involved in gay rights or reproductive choice. In fact, when congregations pulled back from addressing these matters, many solid thoughtful church members, previously concerned about societal issues, seemed to be among the first to drift away. If their congregations were not devoted to causes which they felt to be at the heart of the Christian gospel, why hang around?

Perhaps the time has come to take another look at the diagnosis of the pathology, and thus the treatment of obviously distressed congregations. If the mainline church is to survive its Babylonian captivity, it must find ways to do evangelism and social action simultaneously. The solution may be in seeing both of these functions as the same thing. Evangelism *is* social witness, and social witness *is* evangelism. Both disciplines, however, must be redefined. Evangelism is not to be confused with membership recruitment, and social witness is not to be confused with political action. Membership recruitment and political action are both noble and important ventures, but they are not to be identified with the aforementioned seminal theological functions.

Evangelism Redefined

First, let us consider how evangelism must be redefined. Most congregationally based departments of evangelism are well aware of the classic definition of the term. Evangelism has to do with winning persons to Christ. Definitions developed by denominations have tended to be wordier and a bit more complicated than that, but the gist is obvious. In practice, however, the typical evangelism committee has been engaged in quite a different enterprise. Its task has been to enlist new members for their local churches. Children of church families ordinarily came through a class offered by the minister, or "joined the church" when they reached a certain age. Every now and then an adult would "come forward" to make a confession of faith in Christ at the conclusion of a service or on a day set aside for the reception of new members. The usual case of this sort involved a husband or wife who had married someone already a member of the congregation. Few responders could be regarded as bull moose sinners who needed to be won to Christ or get "saved." There tended to be fewer and fewer adult baptisms.

In pursuit of their practical function, what the evangelism committee actually did was visit persons or families who had previously attended a church service and had filled out a visitor's card, or were otherwise identified as guests. Most of these "prospects" were long-time Christians who had recently moved to town or who were looking for a new church home, having become dissatisfied with the old one. A few had dropped out of the church a few years back and had decided to get in touch with their religious roots now that they had children old enough to be in Sunday school. Another even larger group of prospects came from "kinship and friendship" networks. Birds of either a feather or common blood do tend to flock together.

Committee members who made these home visits knew their agenda and their sales pitch. They had often gone through them during committee meetings in role-play interviews. They would begin their home visits by saying something affirming about the house, a picture, the garden, or the children. Every family member would be addressed by their first names. The dog would be petted and an effort made to get the TV turned off. The visitors made every effort to keep the conversation positive and to elicit "yes" answers to their initial general questions. On no condition did they argue with the prospects or get too deeply involved in religious subjects. Theirs was a friendly church with programs for every family member. Their minister was the finest in the city. Their music program, youth groups, and fellowship groups were more than adequate.

The task was easier and they were much more comfortable making the call when it was clear that the prospects would "fit" comfortably in the congregation. "Our kind of people," they would say to themselves. While they were courteous to those obviously of a different socioeconomic group, the call tended to be a bit awkward. If the person or family being visited had serious religious questions or wanted some information about the Bible or what the church believed, more often than not it was suggested that these were matters for the minister to handle. Visitors rarely carried Bibles, and the handout brochure they brought along tended to described the nature of the church's program, not the nature or the demands of faith.

While the above description may appear to be somewhat of a caricature and not representative of what takes place in many congregations, what I have described is what in fact often happens.

A sizable number of more aggressive congregations have attempted to reach the "unchurched" in their communities by the use of popular marketing tools. Inserts targeted to specific zip codes have been periodically included in the daily paper or distributed in electric bills. One congregation made ten thousand phone calls, covering every address within a mile of the church. To those who responded with even mild interest, five mailings followed, reinforced by two additional phone calls and two personal visits. It was the hope that a new congregation of at least a hundred persons could be developed from those identified as potential prospects. The new fellowship would focus its life around an early Sunday morning worship service held in the church's sanctuary but using "praise" music and a freewheeling liturgical pattern.

Another nearby congregation initiated a series of Saturday noontime jazz concerts on the steps of their downtown church, in hopes of getting a new younger generation just a few feet closer to the building. Still another innovative congregation secured the names and addresses of all new hookups from a local utility, and followed up a mailing with a phone call and, if there was any interest shown, a visit. One aggressive pastor arose before dawn and placed a church invitation in the morning newspaper of each new arrival in town.

Each of these techniques proved to be of value. Only a church with limited imagination, or a death wish, can avoid engaging in some sort of membership recruitment. *But nothing I have just described is evangelism!* Evangelism is not marketing the church. It is proclaiming the gospel—God's good news in Jesus Christ—in word and deed, to the end that men and women may hear, understand, receive, and live it, and be of service in the coming reign of God.

The sickness that seems ubiquitous in the mainline church has come about partly because membership recruitment has replaced evangelism. "Your end of a search for a friendly church" is not the same as "Follow Jesus." What eventuates from most membership recruitment drives tends to be the enlargement of a social group without much religious or theological substance, bound together by friendships and a few common goals, but not much more. In smooth times, that may be enough for many people. But it is an unsheltered windy place to hide in a storm. And at this writing a storm is what mainline churches are facing almost everywhere.

Those looking for more religious substance and for answers to their profound questions may fall subject to the attractive and certain trumpets of fundamentalists of one sort or another. Most of the increasing number of mainline dropouts, however, will be overcome by the secularism out of which they may have emerged. Among the sophisticated, a Sunday morning with the *New York Times* and an elegant brunch meets needs the church doesn't. For baby boomers, busters, and those that follow, a long bike ride, an outing with friends, or just lolling around is a better way to get ready for another long work week. For others it is just an hour to the lake, and no time at all to the backyard swimming pool. Parents who work outside the home need the Sunday morning hours for a variety of chores. Without leadership by their wives, most working-class men do not readily respond to the call of the typical congregation. Few in any of these groups feel the need of a friendly church. In fact, the way religion has been marketed to them, they don't need any church at all. The preferred alternative is not fundamentalism but secularism.

Karen Armstrong, a British feminist and former member of a Catholic religious order, describes the problem:

> A secular society has been slowly evolving which is independent of any Church. Our politics, our education, our "charitable" social work are no longer undertaken as they were for nearly two thousand years by dedicated Christians intent on bringing about the Kingdom of God. It is no longer necessary in England to subscribe to the 39 Articles of the Church

of England to be admitted into Oxford or Cambridge University or into the civil service....Religion, it could be said, has become irrelevant to the mainstream of life in the 20th century, and the fact that many Christian churches are fast being emptied of committed believers shows that Christianity has been pushed to the sidelines because it no longer has anything to say to our liberated and secular world where, in certain parts of society, a lack of Christian belief and a skepticism about conventional religion is often taken for granted and even encouraged (Karen Armstrong, *The Gospel According to Woman*. London: Elm Tree Books, 1986, Preface).

Herein lies the biggest challenge to the future of mainline religion. The threat does not come from the fundamentalists. They are simply trying to fill a vacuum we have created by our lack of theological definition and substance. The question before us is this: "Does the Christian faith have any radical, life-changing, society-reordering word to say in the modern world?" A response to that question is what evangelism must be about.

If there is little hunger for the sort of program, camaraderie, or busyness that tend to be the predominant style of much mainline religion, there is in our society a desperate hunger for a deeply rooted spirituality. The plethora of twelve-step support groups as well as the burgeoning of sectarian evangelical bodies testifies to this hunger. It was not long ago that a generation of young people engaged in a vigorous search for meaning using a variety of encounter groups, meditation rituals, transactional analysis, Eastern religions, EST, Rolfing, a fascination with crystals and pyramids, and a host of other offbeat quasi-religious enterprises. Mainline religion tended to write them off as quirky. Fundamentalists were quicker to read the signs of the times and stepped in with authority. Now mainliners sit around wondering where all the young people have gone. All they need to do is pay a visit to any one of the ubiquitous tabernacles in their communities and they will see where some of them have gone.

The spiritual hunger and the quest for meaning are still present, but the answers most nonreligious younger people are finding are deeply rooted in secular values with spiritual overtones. The environmental movement, for instance, is staffed by those who believe that it, not the religious establishment, is offering a cause worth their time, money, and commitment.

Mainline churches may never meet some of the articulated needs many in modern society seem to have. People want clear, clean, absolute, black and white answers to complicated questions about morality, family life, vocation, the Bible, faith, and the Christian life. Liberal religion has not and cannot meet that need. The religious issues with which we are being confronted are not simply put, and are certainly not simply answered. We do not have a ready supply of verses to be hauled out at a moment's notice in order to provide the last word about much of anything. But we undersell many in our culture if we hold they are unwilling and unprepared to deal with what is more profound than biblical proof texts. An evangelism that expects little, and a religious institution long on program and short on disciplined biblical and theological work, will not endure.

We are not in competition with the popular forms of faith abroad these days. In fact, when religion has been very popular and very conservative, it has been bad news for the world around it. If we continue to despair because we measure success by false standards, we will be continually covered in institutional gloom. For a long time we have said that God did not call us to be successful, but to be faithful. Our problem is not that we don't get out the numbers we used to, or that "they" now do, but that we have allowed a once vital religious institution to devolve into pleasant groups of mostly older people talking about how good things were in the old days, and holding themselves aloof from the biting issues that face the world around them.

In many churches that take the intellectual quality of faith seriously, religion tends to be stuffed up in the head. Theology is not simply a rational enterprise. Information or rational discourse, without experience, is deadly. Even the thoughtful these days are looking for a religious experience, not simply a new set of ideas. While we are called to love God with all our minds, we are also called to love God with all our hearts and souls—and we might add, our bodies.

Theology is not doctrine or the study of doctrine, but the way in which doctrine takes on active experiential meaning. That is why theology must always be contextual. Theology exists not as a Platonic form or idea, but only in relationship to a people, their culture, and the way they understand themselves and the meaning of events. As there are a multiplicity of contexts, so there will be a multiplicity of theologies. Liberation theology, for instance, flows from the day-to-day experience, not the doctrinal analysis, of people living under oppression, who come to realize that God has a preferential option for the poor and is actively engaged with them in securing and celebrating their freedom. If theology could be reduced to doctrinal statements, then for any given language there could be only one accurate and true articulation of the faith, and that articulation need only be literally translated into other languages to be authentic in any given culture.

Even though we have said some harsh things about church growth as ersatz evangelism, we must call men and women, boys and girls to personal faith in God and in Jesus the Christ. I believe the largest group of unchurched persons in most of our communities is made up of those who have long since given up on religion as being superstitious and without meaning for the world in which they live. To find a church that takes them and their questions seriously, and indeed provides a forum in which they can safely explore their doubts, is what they have long been hoping to find.

The rebirth of the mainline church will come when it realizes that it is now sideline, and has a very different function to perform in a society it once controlled. Smaller congregations of highly literate—biblically and theologically—joyful, turned-on, serving people, who know what they believe, and who are teaching their children the songs of Zion, will be prepared for a day whose outlines and shape are not yet clear. Instead of trying to smooth the way by attempting to meet the social needs of those who enter the doors, we will have come to a new and better place when our evangelistic teams suggest that joining the church will seriously alter their priorities. Calling people to a vital faith must be central to the life of the congregation in captivity.

Even though it violated the traditional ways of doing things in my denomination, for years the church I served never offered a public invitation to church membership. Neither did our lay calling teams attempt to get folks signed up during home visits. I would ask that anyone interested in making a confession of faith in Christ and receiving baptism, or transferring their membership, meet with me in my office where I would ask the question, "In what way will becoming part of this church reorder your priorities and change your life?" It was the need of the coming reign of God, not their personal needs, that was at the top of the agenda. Once the answer to that question was reasonably clear, we could proceed to talk about the life-sustaining, joyful, experience-centered discipline that membership in the church required.

Obviously not everyone we encountered was at the same level of readiness. There were those who were only mildly interested in the religious aspects of church membership and came to us because of our program, or because friends encouraged them to join, or because they were simply looking for the kind of church home they had recently left. But slowly the tenor and mind-set of the congregation began to change and evangelism took on a deeper, richer meaning.

Social Witness Redefined

Almost every Christian believes in evangelism, albeit variously defined. These days, however, a shrinking number of those in mainline churches are as committed to social witness, no matter how defined. Many congregations have come to believe that the sort of political and cultural activism popular a generation ago is now counterproductive to the health and growth of the church. While the notion of mission has shifted from projects sponsored by the denominations at home and abroad to causes within local communities, the context has also shifted from institutional reformation to acts of charity.

Congregations are committing ever-increasing percentages of their benevolence and outreach budgets to projects in their own backyards. But on the wane are church structures dedicated to advocacy. Mainline churches seem to be more and more concerned with charity, and less and less concerned with justice. We feed the hungry, but shy away from dealing with the social structures that keep people poor. The passion that captured the attention of the church during the civil rights days has dramatically ebbed. The military-industrial complex is left practically unchallenged by religious structures. While there seems to be an increasing sensitivity to victims of AIDS, most of our congregations, as well as our denominational and interchurch structures, hold issues facing gay and lesbian people at arm's length. The Metropolitan Community Church is still being denied admission to the family of communions that constitute the National Council of Churches. While we have managed to clean up the formerly sexist language of our hymnals and books of worship, the reaction to the interdenominational conference on "Re-Imaging," describes a religious community deeply divided about matters important to many women.

In the meantime, food kitchens, shelters for the homeless, clothing outlets, and day-care centers abound. While these local enterprises are of value and ought to be part of the program of mainline congregations, they should not be confused with social witness. Charity deals with the needs of individuals. Social witness deals with the structures that make charity necessary. Charity deals with the symptoms. Social witness deals with the underlying pathology. Charity begins in the church's emergency room. Social justice begins in the church's laboratory.

There are two apparent reasons why social justice concerns are being played *soto voce* in the mainline church. First, in recent years there may have developed an unreflective relationship between liberal politics and social justice issues. While we must admit to more than an occasional correlation, the agenda of the Democratic Party is not identical with the demands of the Christian gospel. While people of liberal political persuasions and goodwill fought on behalf of the poor, the dispossessed, the pariahs, and were deeply moved by arguments for human rights, they were not equally committed to responsibilities. Despite liberal rhetoric, the United States and other nations with elaborate welfare programs succeeded in developing a sturdy army of people who believed that society owed them a living, and who had discovered sophisticated methods to get it without having to exercise any responsibility or attempt to work their way out of their persistent problems. While there are mean-spirited, selfish, and unrelenting political conservatives, there are others across the political spectrum who differ with the classic liberals only in terms of means. The more profoundly the mainline establishment was committed to ignoring those with a more conservative economic bent, the greater the hiatus between their churches and the American people at large. No political party has a monopoly on either common sense or an adequate understanding of the Christian gospel.

The second reason for the diminution of social witness ministries among the mainline churches arose from the opposite direction. The less theologically and biblically equipped church members were, the more they took their bearings from secular sources. It was often difficult to tell the difference between church members views on significant social matters, and those of nonmembers. In fact, some religionists even within mainline churches made common cause with the most repressive forces in secular society. That is nothing new. From the Inquisition to slavery, religion has often been more part of the problem than the solution. Nowhere was segregation held onto more tenaciously than in the church of the American South. And when that system had been successfully challenged practically everywhere else, it was still true that eleven o'clock Sunday morning was the most segregated hour of the week. Upon what bases were these ideological idiocies formed? From theological perspectives that used a verse of scripture here and a verse of scripture there to prove what a secular culture had already decided was to be the prevailing ethos. One should not be too ready to mimic the successful religious conservatives, or even to be enamored of their increasing popularity. When religion has been very popular, it has tended to support the least just and most oppressive forces within society.

To the extent the mainline church has allowed itself to be diluted by those whose theological posture is not only immature but also horribly distorted, it has lost the heart of the gospel. Those who fail to understand the nature of evangelism may be equally as unaware of the nature of the Christian social witness.

Evangelism/Social Witness and the Coming Reign of God

The redefinition of evangelism and the redefinition of the church's social witness point in the same direction and end up at the same place. The meaning of each depends on how one understands the church. And that is perhaps our most pressing theological question.

In the Gospel record there is practically nothing from the lips of Jesus about the church. The two uses of the word are no doubt later additions to the text. Jesus did, however, talk extensively about the reign of God he had come to herald. (For a fuller discussion of this subject see *Building a Biblical Faith*, Chapter Eight). The church is not the kingdom or reign of God. It is a human institution. At best it is an intimation, a foretaste, a demonstration project, an advanced party of the reign of God—a beachhead of the authority that is to come. It describes by what it is and what it does how the Kingdom might look.

It is God who brings the Kingdom to earth as it is in heaven. The church only prays for the day when that will happen. The church reaches into the future and lives out what is to be in the here and now. If the church exists in the world, it is not of the world. The way it operates, the rules under which it lives, the ethic it espouses tend to be very different than the rules and the ethic of the secular world. Practically every parable attributed to Jesus makes that point.

It is not that someday all the world will be in the church, but that the church—the reign of God—will be in all the world. The fullness of God's reign will be realized when "The kingdoms of this world become the Kingdom of our Lord, and of his Christ, and God shall reign forever and ever." The church's task is to share with God in the work of reconciling all things, things in heaven and things on earth, to God. The cross is the primary symbol of God's atoning work.

Both evangelism and social witness can therefore be defined as the proclamation of the evangel, the reconciling work of God in Christ. The church proclaims; God reconciles.

Evangelism is not winning souls or enlarging the membership of the church. Evangelism is the proclamation of the evangel. Social witness is not doing acts of charity or seeking to alter the political systems. It is rather a demonstration within the unredeemed world as to how society will look when the reign of God is fully established. Evangelism and social witness are simply two ways to do the same thing. Both are acted out in the world beyond the church. Both testify as to how God's reign will be shaped. While we tend to think of evangelism as being addressed to individuals and social witness as addressed to culture, whichever word we use points to the same reality.

Even during the duration of its current captivity, the mainline church cannot hibernate or collapse into itself. Its life is always to be lived out in the world, for that is the locus of Christ's mission. The way the church lives in the world, however, is of critical importance. It can never be too comfortable in Babylon. Even though it seems trapped by fundamentalisms—religious and political—on one side, and rampant secularism on the other, it remains clear about the reconciling gospel it is called to proclaim in word and deed.

Unless those who constitute its membership, clergy and lay, are theologically well grounded and biblically literate, the church will have little to say anyone needs to hear. If it succumbs to finding success in its own version of fundamentalism, it will have become just another sectarian sport, out of touch with the world to which it ministers. If it succumbs to secularism, it will have lost the gospel. The greatest danger facing the mainline church is that as its institutional strength continues to ebb, leaders both at the denominational and the congregational levels will attempt to save it by mimicking either an easy secularism or a strident evangelicalism under the rubric, "If you can't lick them, then join them." The narrow passage between Scylla and Charybdis is achieved only by the disciplined. Neither will the mainline church survive if it divides its ranks between those dedicated to church growth and those dedicated to political action. Rather, each congregation must see itself as a reconciling community whose evangelistic and social witness tasks are identical.

Rethinking Congregational Structures

We have insisted throughout this book that reflection and action are inseparable. Institutions that spend enormous amounts of effort restructuring themselves, without a sufficient ideological basis for the modifications, engage in frantic activity that may occupy their attention but which tends to be unproductive. Likewise, institutions that have it all thought out, but do not engage in the hard work of realigning their internal systems, tend to end up about where they started. There are church bodies that have redone their organizational charts every few years without solving any of their major problems. There are also church bodies that periodically rewrite their mission statements but never develop the necessary implementing structures.

Most mainline congregations are organized around committees, task forces, working groups, or divisions that report to an elected administrative body known as the board, vestry, council, session, or some similar identification. These small working units traditionally divide the functions of the congregation programmatically. Thus education, social witness, and evangelism follow quite separate tracks. Their work is coordinated as they report to an administrative body, or board. But their agendas tend to be very different, and they employ the skills and time of people with very different religious sensitivities. Thus evangelism and social witness are not thought of as the same enterprise—the proclamation of the evangel.

Consider an alternative congregational structure, which sees evangelism and social witness as inseparable. Since it is a term with some currency, we will call the new units "ministries." Under the terms of this alternative administrative format, the program of the congregation is organized around a common understanding of the previously defined mission. The church is committed to proclaiming the evangel in word and deed. Everything must meet the test of that simple affirmation. Having defined its mission, the congregation organizes its life around it.

Each of the various ministries is first of all an educational unit. It meets weekly, perhaps on Sunday morning, replacing the traditional church school class, or perhaps at some other convenient time. Several of the ministries may decide to gather on the same evening. If so, the meeting time is divided into three parts. First, the resident theologian, the minister in most cases, offers an in-depth biblical and theological study, which relates to the articulated mission of the congregation. This will be done as all the ministries are in joint session. The second part of the period is dedicated to the way the individual ministries deal with the relationship between their particular tasks and the theological and biblical material just covered. The third part of the session involves taking care of the necessary nuts-and-bolts functions of the individual ministries.

Consider the following example as to how a congregational structure can be transformed to serve a commonly agreed-upon understanding of the church's mission.

For some years Willow Street Church had been engaged in a housing ministry for elderly people on limited incomes. An eighty-unit apartment complex was constructed adjacent to the church building. The project was completed with the assistance of the denomination and a government-guaranteed low-interest loan. While a handful of residents are aware of the church connection, there is little contact between the apartment residents and the congregation. No way has been generated to identify and care for the spiritual needs of the elderly residents who can no longer get to church. New residents, who may not be mobile, do not see themselves as potential members of the congregation. The committee responsible for the apartment is a subgroup of the larger division of social witness. It is essentially a house and grounds committee concerned with providing the residents transportation to the store, and making sure the grass gets cut and the roof repaired. Now and then someone from the congregation's evangelism committee will call on an apartment resident who has visited the worship service for the first time. There is no official contact between this group and the group that operates the facility, other than that they both report to the congregation's administrative board.

Consider how the congregation might reconfigure its structure so that the church more self-consciously lives out its articulated mission. If the evangelism committee and the social witness committee are both self-consciously concerned about the same thing—the proclamation of the good news of God in Jesus Christ—then not only can their efforts be combined, but also their structures. Assume that a reconstituted body responsible for this "ministry" meets on Sunday mornings prior to the worship service. Several of these ministries have agreed to gather at the same time, having replaced the old adult church school classes. The minister leads in a thirty-minute in-depth Bible study and theological lesson before the combined group. Coffee and donuts are provided by one of the ministries. Each ministry then assembles in its assigned area to discuss how the lesson relates to its particular function. There follows a working session growing out of what was just discussed.

During this third part of their meeting, the action plan for the housing ministry includes the following current concerns:

- The lonely fears and sense of isolation of four newer residents, identified by ministry members who make regular visits to the building.
- The leak in the roof.
- An offer by a fundamentalist congregation to conduct regular Bible studies for the residents.
- A decision pending before the federal government to cut back on resources dedicated to housing for the elderly and the poor.
- How to prepare a half-dozen newer residents for membership in the congregation.

Twelve similar ministries make up the basic programmatic structure of Willow Street Church. The administrative board coordinates these ministries and handles that part of the program that cannot easily be located in one of the ministries. However, what cannot be done within an action/reflection ministry tends to be eliminated from the program of the congregation. Special groups are set up under the board's direction to deal with bookkeeping, repairs, personnel matters, and similar routine functions. But the energy of the congregation is not consumed in matters that have little relationship to the mission statement and thus to the ministries that grow out of it.

There are obviously variations on this system. The point, however, is always the same: the life, work, and ministry of the congregation revolves around its articulated mission. The mission grows out of a self-conscious theological rationale. Instead of being at odds, the central functions of the church—in this case evangelism and social witness—are seen as identical concerns implemented by the same programmatic structure.

What the Congregation Expects of Its Members

In many mainline congregations a handful of the members do most of the work. Beyond this inner circle of "pillars" there is usually another group that can be counted on from time to time. These two sets of doers are surrounded by yet another larger group of people who enjoy coming to worship, or participating as listeners in some other aspect of the church's life, but cannot be counted on to help execute the mission. Since they made no such commitment when they first joined the church, they are doing only what they first agreed to do—or not to do.

While that problem cannot be fully or easily resolved in any unit of society, it is becoming increasingly clear that given the current set of circumstances, the mainline church will not survive its captivity with enough residual power to meet the challenges of Babylon, or to emerge from it with sufficient strength when history cycles to a better place.

Two other structural modifications, therefore, must be put in place from the outset.

First, people are not admitted to the church's membership until they have agreed to participate in the biblical/theological courses that have become the core of the congregation's educational life. In fact, it would be better if formal membership was not granted until the courses were completed.

Second, every member of the church physically or emotionally able to do so is automatically, by virtue of membership, part of one of the ministries. Outside the membership there may be a significant number of people who come to listen. Inside the membership, however, there are only the committed. Every member is enlisted in extending the congregation's mission and sharing in the evangelistic/social witness agenda, which is the proclamation of the evangel—the good news of God's redemptive reconciling love in Jesus Christ.

It may be argued that requiring such a commitment will surely diminish the size of the membership. Anyone who worries about that problem hasn't looked around lately. Few groups in society, including those dedicated to religious causes, receive more from their constituents than they require. The most vital churches in our midst are those with high expectations of all who share the faith. The fearful, who have become enamored with a variety of church growth techniques, have often tended to forsake depth and meaning and to ask for little from those they seek to enlist. Given current dynamics, that stance is a death wish. If anything will kill off a captive church, it is the increased dilution of its message and a playing down of its call to commitment.

Increasing numbers of mainline congregations are dying every day. A look through the yearbooks of any of our denominations also will turn up long lists of formerly strong churches that now stay alive only by virtue of endowments, or a few grand old saints who just refuse to give up. But the church exists to be more than an ecclesiastical nursing home. It exists to call the world's attention to God's reconciling love, and to perform, on God's behalf, ministries of reconciliation. Short of that commitment, congregations might have little cause to exist and therefore may fall under judgment. At this writing history seems hard at work executing that judgment.

Questions for Reflection and Discussion

1. In your congregation, how are the evangelistic responsibilities and the social witness responsibilities divided administratively? In what ways do those assigned to each task have differing perspectives?

2. In an age of diminishing resources, how are priorities for congregational expenditures determined? Over the past few years has social witness suffered because the major emphasis was on evangelism, or was it the other way around? How were these decisions made?

3. The thrust of membership recruitment and church growth is toward the congregation—bringing outsiders in. The thrust of evangelism is toward the world—the proclamation of the gospel. How are these tasks divided in your congregation, or are they seen as identical? What are the structures and programs that focus on church growth and membership recruitment, and what are the structures that center on evangelism?

4. There are, no doubt, a variety of groups and organizations in your community whose goal it is to meet the inner needs of persons. Some of these organizations are churches, but others are twelve-step groups or meditation societies. What do they offer many people, assuming the churches do not? What can we learn from them?

5. Most of our congregations are increasingly committed to meeting human needs: food, clothing, and shelter. List all the charitable projects in which the churches of your community engage. Now list the projects that ask the question, "Why are they hungry?" How does a congregation move from charity to justice? Or is justice only a political concern about which the church has little to offer?

6. How does the religious community engage in the call for justice without becoming captive of somebody else's political program?

7. If somehow evangelism and social witness are the same thing, define how congregational structures can be modified so that these aspects of church life are not seen as antithetical, or even significantly different.

8. The evangelistic task is never completed until the fruits of the Christ life are evident in those who have been evangelized. What are the expectations placed on new members in your congregation?

9 | The Communion of Saints

Much of what we have thus far described may seem harsh, cold and overly committed to discipline, academic stringency, and just plain hard work. While it is true that the survival of the mainline church depends on a tough new level of commitment, we come in this chapter to a warmer, heartfelt aspect of our survival strategy. We are not just dealing with programs, doctrines, and structures. We are talking about people—flesh-and-blood, emotionally sensitive, potentially joyful, more than occasionally broken human beings, whose need of one another defines an essential part of their physical and spiritual natures. Theology cannot be done without reference to persons, and therefore seldom done outside a community of faith. The Spirit is often within us, but always among us.

Intimate Communities in an Anonymous Culture

In our mobile society it is difficult to build closely knit communities of faith. There was a day when the church dominated the social system of the neighborhood and a sense of community was built in. Everyone knew everyone else, and there was the discipline of that fundamental connection. An ethical standard was at least expected of the congregation's members. Marriage within the congregation was not the exception; it was the rule. More than occasionally the church lived under the direction of two or three extended families. As long as these clans were at peace, all was well. When a struggle over property, power, or some offense—real or imagined— put these families at odds, the entire congregation was in turmoil.

Children were reared not only within their nuclear families, but also by other members of the congregation, and by the neighbors. While there are exceptions, especially in small or rural communities, today's mainline congregation tends to include an assorted collection of relative strangers. Not only can we live cheek to jowl in an urban apartment complex with people whose names we never know, but we can sit next to them in church and not have the faintest notion as to who they are or what their world is like.

There was a day when it was impossible for a child to be born and not have most members of the church acknowledge the event, probably with a house call. Back doors were unlocked and open, and the kitchen of one family was a potential sitting room and coffee shop for anyone on the block. A child playing on the sidewalk was the responsibility of every neighbor up and down the street. Today few people are likely to be home after school or on weekends, and even if they were, what happens to that child is nobody's business. It was not that long ago that one could count on three generations all being within walking distance. These days in many urban centers, even funerals are held in private. Family members are shunted into a side room where they are not seen, thus hiding their tears but reinforcing their isolation.

The old days are gone, never to return, and with their passing has come a diminished role for the congregation as the arbiter of the social structure. What the leaders of the church said once had enormous authority; now nobody takes much notice. Once, information flowed quickly, since everyone was regularly in everyone else's residence. In communities where I have recently lived, not even the pastor dares visit a home without having made an appointment, and what has happened within those walls is a fiercely guarded secret. Of course, every congregation has within it well-defined circles of close friends. Even today more lifelong commitments are made by those who share the same pew than in any other social structure.

There are religious bodies that work hard at recreating a more intimate world within the larger culture where we tend to hold each other at arm's length. One of the appeals of certain sectarian groups, the Mormons being a good example, is that they say to those uncomfortable in this culture, "We will be your family." And indeed they are. No one is unknown or uncared for. No one is allowed to suffer silently. No one's life is a closed book. If in much of the contemporary urban world the hectic pace of life is rightfully protected from such openness, in the process certain human values are compromised.

Even so, churches still have a head start over every other social institution in building intimate communities of mutual trust and support. Among less affluent young families, all trying to get their feet on the ground in a competitive culture, there is often an intimacy and a sharing that gets them through the tough years. Children's beds passed from one to the other as the need arises, simple meals shared in homes, mutual baby-sitting for the occasional night out, vacations together on the cheap—all are part of the remarkable sense of community that identifies informal clusters of friends found at church.

And yet, too many are left out. I have often observed after-worship coffee hours that looked all the world like a collection of football huddles, with odd couples and singles left on the outside to fend for themselves and to do whatever they could with their growing sense of exclusion and loneliness.

Perhaps the individualism and privatization of daily living has reached a point of no return, and a day is about to dawn in which the pendulum may begin to swing back. If so, it will be a recommitment to more authentic forms of church life. It was never intended that the church be a collection of isolated individuals each doing his or her own thing. Neither is the church an audience consisting of a diverse assortment of spectators, each of whom comes for his or her own amusement. The church, at its best, is a body in which every part has a clear organic relationship to every other part. Culture these days may worship independence, but the church is always an interdependent community. We are members of one another, not just part of a voluntary association of individuals whose actions, ethics, and faith have no fundamental bearing on each other's lives.

The Communion of Saints 133

If the sense of body is important to the church in less constricted times, how much more important does it become during periods of captivity? However, there is a thin line that we must approach with considerable caution, lest we become secluded knots of people who cling to each other, but disdain the world in which we live. That is the path to sectarianism. Interdependence is not the same as a rejection of the rest of society. Yet perhaps the shortcoming of the mainline church is not that we have distanced ourselves from the world, but that we tend to be of, by, and for it, as well as simply in it.

Increasingly both adults and their children draw their ethics, values, and commitments more regularly from almost every other corner of their social networks than they do from their communities of faith. If to be baptized is in some sense to be set apart, we have lost much of that realization. A recovery of the sacred will not come from doctrine learned, but from lives shared. In a body we not only hold each other accountable, but the actions of any member also impact the lives of every other member.

> Blest be the tie that binds our hearts in Christian love,
> The fellowship of kindred minds is like to that above.
> John Fawcett

New Forms of Cooperative Living

While the single-family unit living to itself will continue to be a powerful norm among members of mainline churches, there is increasing room for models of cooperative living. These new constellations may go far beyond friends who spend time together and who share hedge trimmers and baby strollers. The joint use of sporadically used equipment may be a good place to begin, but it only scratches the surface of economically sound and spiritually sustaining living arrangements. There are more extensive models that churches can instigate, bless, and monitor.

An ecumenical congregation I served some years ago on the campus of the University of Chicago has established a number of new forms of intra-congregational living. For example, some time back a large-abandoned apartment building in a seriously blighted area a few blocks from the church building was purchased. A dozen families agreed to move into it, after rehabilitating their own private space. In formal real estate terms, what became known as "The Covenantal

Community" was a cooperative apartment. The building was jointly owned, with each family securing space from the church corporation that managed the entire project. In time the group purchased land outside the city on which to grow their own table vegetables and use as a retreat from the harshness of inner-urban life. Applicants who were not church members were invited to enter the community so that eventually there was a rich mixture of persons of various races, ethnic heritages and family constellations. Children growing up in The Covenantal Community, which is now almost twenty years old and far more extensive than the original small group experiment, have a richer, very different sense of the fellowship of the church.

A number of years ago my wife and I bought, with another couple from the church we most recently served, a large, empty, dilapidated Victorian home near our downtown area. We rehabilitated it with our own hands and a little outside expert help. It had formerly been used as a duplex. We took out part of the middle wall to make one marvelous kitchen. We shared a dining room and a library. Each couple had its our upstairs bedrooms and downstairs living room. We divided the expenses for groceries, and jointly paid all other household bills. Most evening meals were eaten together using a flexible rotating cooking schedule. With the money we saved, my wife and I were able to fund rather extensive summer trips. Beyond the anticipated economic windfall, we wanted to demonstrate that there are a variety of ways within the Christian framework to live in an urban culture overly protective of personal privacy.

Generating Inclusive Models of Family Life

Many of us have become increasingly concerned about the breakdown of the traditional family. No one can doubt that families are in crisis. The passion to affirm family values is both a timely and a necessary corrective in a secular world. However, at least part of the problem lies in a much too narrow definition of the word "family." In most churches there are far more people present on a given Sunday morning who live outside a traditional family system composed of Mom, Dad, and the kids, than within one. If you don't believe it, just make a count. Any talk, therefore, about family values automatically leaves most folk out. The Chinese pictograph for crisis is composed of two figures—danger and opportunity. We are all aware of the danger in the current crisis over family values. But consider the opportunities.

What better combination of both resources and needs can one imagine than the lonely older couple whose grandchildren are far away, becoming close friends with children whose grandparents are just as distant!

Few may feel more isolated and out of place in our society than the single parent. Many mothers are already under or feel under judgment for having a child or multiple children without husbands. Others are doing their best to recover from difficult and now disintegrated marriages or relationships. Raising children is hard work at best. Raising children alone following a treacherous life passage is even more demanding. If anyone needs a community of faith, it is the single parent. But these people often find it awkward to sense much acceptance in churches that continually talk about family values, and by that mean the classic nuclear family. Yet the church must be an institution that is able to affirm without condition the otherwise marginalized.

Another significant population, many of whose members feel beyond the blessing of most mainline congregations, is composed of gay and lesbian persons, either open or closeted, living alone or as couples. Yet the church may be the one major player in modern society that is ideologically able to move beyond the homophobia that otherwise infects the culture. The church has often played a strategic role in breaking down walls of ignorance and prejudice on behalf of the pariahs and disenfranchised. The impact of religion in staffing, funding, and providing the moral imperative in the civil rights struggle of a generation ago, may in our era be replicated on behalf of homosexuals.

The time may be ripe for the traditional "Wedding Ring Sunday School Class" to give way to an evangelistic—as we have defined it—intergenerational ministry, which includes in its ranks persons from a great variety of family structures. We no longer live in a culture of Mom, Dad, and the kids, with grandparents near at hand. Yet most people need an intimate framework that replicates at least some of the values found in that constellation. Where is it to be found if not in the church? While there is often great value in singles groups within the church, these organizations may actually further isolate the unmarried or the previously married. Many singles with whom I have talked recite the frustration inherent in looking for safe, comfortable, undemanding acceptance in the typical singles bar or even the typical single church group. But that richness can be found in many solid mainline congregations, which have learned to welcome a great variety of people in their mainstream.

Having "Some" Things in Common

Very early in the life of the Christian movement an experiment was attempted in which members of the church held "all things in common." Outside the passage in Acts 2, which makes note of this development, it is never heard of again until the rise of monasticism. For a variety of reasons the church apparently gave up the notion of communal property almost as soon as it was attempted. While the ideal society might be one that operates under the rubric, "From each according to ability, to each according to need," we are not likely to see any wide-scale redevelopment of that model in the modern church. And yet, the reduction of economics to "everyone for themselves, and the devil take the hindmost" seems far removed from what the reign of God might look like were it to fully come. Is it possible to more nearly model the Kingdom while being realistic about how things operate in this world? If we cannot have all things in common, is it possible to have some things in common, or at least to strive for a more equitable distribution of things? While this image may be thought socially impossible, to the extent the church is a demonstration of what the reign of God will look like, we might find new ways to move in that direction.

Examples abound. There are congregations whose members do cooperative buying of staples and other household products. In many places families informally share a variety of household items as needs come and go. Other churches have out-of-town cabins for use by their families for weekend retreats or short vacations. The ubiquitous church bus is most often seen as property held in common. The church building itself belongs to and is used by everyone. We probably already do far more sharing than may be obvious. These simple matters may just scratch the surface of what might happen in a congregation that has arrived at new levels of interpersonal responsibility and intimacy.

"From each according to ability" may mean fresh ways to think about stewardship. In most mainline congregations, who has what and who gives what is nobody's business. For most of my years as a local pastor I was scrupulous in my avoidance of examining the records of individual giving. I just didn't want to know who contributed how much. I was also insistent that nobody else knew, outside the officials who posted the records. This information was safely in the computer where it remained locked behind coded passwords. I felt that a personal knowledge of giving records might prejudice my ability to be an evenhanded pastor. More than that, economic privatism is built into the social fabric, and therefore I, as someone highly conditioned by society, felt financial privacy to be essential. One's sex life and one's income are nobody else's business. I might have itched to know, but it seemed that the risks of knowing were larger than the benefits. Things could get very sticky. Look at what happened to Ananias and Sapphira, whose deaths seemed to have been caused by snoopy church officers.

Must we in the Christian community really be that isolated and self-contained? There may be a larger sense in which we need to hold one another accountable. The closest we come to it is in charts used during financial campaigns to show various levels of giving, given a range of income levels. When I finally decided to look at the contribution records I became a much better pastor. Not only did I sense how spiritual needs and financial resources tended to be related, but I also was provided with many valuable clues as to problems of faith within the membership of the church. It is still true that treasure and heart seem to occupy the same spiritual territory. How congregations go about effecting the "from each according to ability" side of the equation is a matter for each church to work through. The need to do it is increasingly apparent, the more deeply the mainline church is mired in Babylon.

Just as serious a concern is the other half of the equation: "to each according to need." While most churches seem to be aware of the economic plight of the poor within their communities, often there is not the same concern about critical needs within the congregation. What happens in a church when a middle-class family's chief breadwinner loses her or his job, and is not reemployed for a year? If somebody's house burns down, we know what to do. If somebody is fired, we are not as certain. Until the United States establishes a comprehensive system for funding health care, there will be those anonymous persons all around us who need to have their teeth fixed or should be visiting a physician, or can't afford lifesaving medicines.

Churches often think of themselves as family. But when it comes to economic needs, the notion tends to fade. If church is family, then it must discover ways to know about everyone's need, and to respond. This community of concern automatically reacts in times of crisis. It becomes immediately obvious that far deeper levels of intimacy and caring mean an awareness and response to anyone in the family in serious trouble. And that requires more basic information about who we are and what we are suffering than is normally the case. While we may not find a way to have all things in common, we can certainly move toward congregational structures in which we have some things in common.

Being Present at the Major Life-changing Moments

Smaller, more intimate congregations seem better equipped to deal with the major life-changing moments in the lives of their members. They tend to be particularly sensitive to births, weddings, and funerals. The fact that each of these three is most often accompanied by an appropriate liturgical ritual gives the church an automatic role. Even so, in urban communities and in larger congregations there is less often the sense that the entire community is part of the event.

What of those times when something happens that does not elicit a formal response by the church? We have already mentioned the loss of a job. There are other occasions where our awkwardness is apparent: divorce, retirement, a criminal conviction, teenage pregnancy, the onset of Alzheimer's, the discovery of an adulterous relationship, failure in school, angry church families at each other's throats, a bitter political disagreement, alcoholism, drug addiction, compulsive gambling or eating, racist attitudes. Each of these life-changing situations presents the church with an occasion to demonstrate whether it is in fact a family, or just employs the verbiage. I know congregations that believe themselves to be very friendly. They greet visitors warmly, and try to fit new members and prospective members into compatible social circles. But let one of these more difficult matters

The Communion of Saints 139

hit, and friendliness turns to recrimination and gossip.

This chapter is about "koinonia" which is usually translated "fellowship." But the Greek word is also translated "participation." The same word is used when describing the Lord's Supper, the Eucharist. The "communion" of saints is more than an awareness that we are surrounded at the table by all those who have gone before. It is at this most profound time when members of the gathered family know they belong to each other. Instead of being a quiet, little, private moment with Jesus, at heart the Lord's Supper is the reconciling and healing moment of the community, where Jesus is present as the one who makes peace and heals wounds. He is within each, but among all.

> We shares each other's woes,
> Each other's burdens bear,
> And often for each other flows
> The sympathizing tear.
> John Fawcett

While everything we have discussed in this chapter rightly belongs within the life of a congregation regardless of the societal circumstances, during this particular era the need for more tightly drawn communities of faith is even more apparent. If we continue to believe that church growth techniques will get us beyond the current difficult place, we will only continue to dilute congregational life. These techniques will not stop the decline, and at the same time they will persist in moving us even farther from the theological integrity and the discipline needed to hold mainline churches together until the tide turns.

In the last few chapters we have reviewed most of the activities usually found in the life of the typical mainline congregation: ministerial leadership, Christian education, worship, evangelism, social witness, administration, stewardship, and community building. We have not discussed the management of the property or other building needs. There is really nothing new I have to say about those matters, except to remind my readers that buildings were made for churches, not churches for buildings.

In the next chapter we will turn to the rapidly changing role of mainline denominations.

Questions for Reflection and Discussion

1. Sometimes congregations are intimate communities where members depend on one another for the meeting of many profound needs. Sometimes members of congregations hardly know each other's names. Describe your congregation now. Compare it to an earlier age—even twenty years ago. If the churches are no longer meeting needs for intimacy, where are people getting those needs met?

2. Are there ways in which congregations can more adequately address issues of isolation and loneliness, now common in most communities? In your congregation are there insiders and outsiders, and what are the self-conscious efforts to meet the needs of the latter?

3. How does your congregation respond to new forms of shared living—two or more families in the same structure, co-ops, single people sharing space?

4. Whether anyone knows it or not, every congregation probably has within it persons who happen to be gay or lesbian. What happens in your congregation when it becomes known? Are people welcomed and affirmed, or isolated and pushed out?

5. Is there an openness in your church in which sharing goods or holding some things in common is not only allowed but celebrated? What about a cooperative buying club—just for a starter?

6. How does your congregation respond at times of birth, marriage, illness, death, retirement, divorce, runaway children, unwanted pregnancies, and the other life crises your members face?

10 | Are Denominations Out of Date?

As the mainline church has continued its precipitous slide into what many think might be ultimate oblivion, powerful and persistent voices have challenged the continued viability of denominations and denominationalism. The argument is made, with increasing effectiveness, that the day of denominations is over, and that local congregations are now the only manifestation of the church that can or should persist. A sturdy collection of cynics hold that no one needs to kill off denominations, because given decreased funding they will eventually just wither and die.

The Declining Power of Denominations

Denominations are accused of perpetuating useless bureaucracies that continue to drain off funds critically needed to support the frontline work of local churches. If the mission of the church was formerly thought of as spanning the oceans with the story of Jesus, today the major mission field lies within the parish boundaries of almost every congregation. Denominations might have been necessary during the expansionist era of mainline Protestantism, but today they are seen as excess baggage. They played a significant role during an era when the focus of missions was on the not-yet-Christians. They have little to say or be in an era dedicated to a witness among the no-longer-Christians. There are those who hold that all the denominational machinery could be levitated out of existence, and the life, faith, and witness of the average parish member would be unaffected. In those denominations where the congregation has the final say as to how its money is spent, less and less of it goes to anything beyond its own city limits. Who hasn't heard it said, "We've got to take care of things here at home first, and then we can think about helping out elsewhere"?

One has only to look around to discover that many of the most powerful congregations in almost every community are relatively, if not entirely, free of denominational ties. Recent years have witnessed the spawning of mega-churches that are virtually one-congregation denominations. Others tend to be aligned with loosely knit national groups, which have nothing to say and little to add to local programs. Each pastor is his own bishop, and is ultimately responsible to no one beyond herself.

Small or modestly sized communities of faith—so the argument goes—may need the resources and the expertise that come from denominational leaders, but thriving churches may not. A small church that calls a minister probably can use all the help it can get to find the right person. A really big church can often identify, negotiate with, and capture the person it wants. All it must do is convince the person that she or he has been "called" to the congregation. To be called seems very different than being assigned by some ecclesiastical official. In systems where a bishop appoints ministers, the problem is ameliorated. And yet even among United Methodists there is increasing agitation about how appointments are handled. Local churches, which have a larger stake in these appointments or methods of "call," are demanding a greater say in the selection of their ministerial leaders.

Not only is a stubborn sense of independence commonplace among evangelical or charismatic churches, it is also increasingly seen in mainline churches. An official in an Australian mainline denomination lamented to me that the largest and strongest congregations in his communion were essentially independent of the parent body. Not only did they have their own community-based mission points, but they trained, funded, and sent missionary partners to several foreign nations—all without denominational support or endorsement. Members of the congregations in question were up front about their allegiance to the denomination, but didn't think it necessary to go through all the mechanical work it took to get done what they could do themselves much more quickly and efficiently.

Several denominations, including the Australian one just alluded to, have been partly responsible for the problem by including in their official statements references to the "autonomy of the congregation." My own communion, the Christian Church (Disciples of Christ), has often prided itself on our commitment to congregational autonomy. We have also talked about the autonomy of the church at regional and general levels, but down in the trenches it is congregational autonomy that gets the greatest cheers.

It is puzzling how any church that claims to take its direction from the New Testament can conclude that any part of the body is a "law to itself." Both Paul and the Christians centered in Jerusalem believed that no part of the body was independent of the whole body. The eye could never say to the hand, "I have no need of you." That, however, is what the two Greek roots that make up the word "autonomy" mean: *auto*=self, *nomos*=law. The American frontier was settled by people who didn't want anybody from New York or Philadelphia, let alone from England or the Continent, telling them what to do. Not only were their political systems largely shaped by this "American" notion, but their ecclesial systems were as well. The idea, however, finds little support in scripture or in the history of the church.

New Roles for Mainline Denominations

I would argue that not only are denominational structures important, but that during this present period when the mainline church is being squeezed dry between secularism on one hand and sectarianism on the other, associations of congregations play a particularly important role. That role, however, may be much different than it has been in recent history. The new role calls for leaders with different skills and a radically reordered sense of the mission of the whole church.

As program planners and managers, denominational structures are increasingly obsolete. Neither do they have a significant role yet to play in what has been called "home missions." Congregations and clusters of congregations know the home mission scene far better and should be called upon to do what needs to be done. The most expensive way to do mission work in the United States is to organize and monitor it from New York, Cleveland, or Indianapolis. In this case the conservative political maxim probably holds, "The most effective government is the government closest to the people."

It is also unclear why denominations need to maintain offices to do what is essentially the function of the congregation. The day is coming when we will do without departments of evangelism, Christian education, stewardship, women's work, men's work, etc., etc., etc. If these national structures no longer serve economically justifiable purposes, the case is even stronger at the judicatory level. In the judicatory with which I am most intimately acquainted, there have for many years been structures paralleling those found in congregations: evangelism, social witness, education, etc. There has in recent years been a struggle to put together agendas worth the time of those who travel from throughout the state to attend the meetings. To bring people together from a number of far-flung communities because it happens to be the second Tuesday of the month is an insufficient reason. We will return to the revitalized function of the judicatory.

Some other tasks that have been performed by denominations are basically administrative. There are pension funds, publishing houses, homes for the aged, pools of money for new buildings, historical records to be kept, money to be raised for purposes beyond the work of congregations, ecumenical relationships to be maintained, and legal issues to be addressed. These activities are beyond the scope of any congregation. Where possible these important national boards should be combined into two or three major units. However, putting corporate bodies together, even administrative units within the same national church, is a tricky business. When three well-paid executives realize that there will be only one left after the restructuring, all sorts of reasons emerge as to why the plan is premature or unworkable.

That problem will eventually be solved by economics. Congregations will sooner or later find ways not to pay for what is not essential. The best administrators and business persons we can find, probably from the laity, should be secured to operate these units.

While I believe that the main task of the local pastor is to be a theologian, not an administrator, I do not belittle the ministry of administration. We need top-notch business heads to perform the sorts of vital functions to which we have just alluded.

Another set of extra congregational functions has to do with servicing the needs of the local units. Materials must be written and printed, deputations engaged in to promote the work of the church beyond the congregation, buildings planned for and designed, conventions and assemblies held—albeit with less frequency. However, when congregations make use of these services they should pay for them. Perhaps private organizations that offer their services for a fee might replace denominational bureaucracies that operate on "mission" money.

The one programmatic task that probably needs to be maintained at the denominational level involves the church's world witness. No denomination is an island, entire to itself. These days the overseas mission of the church does not involve taking the gospel to "pagan" lands as much as entering into fraternal relationships with maturing churches elsewhere in the world. Perhaps missions has become purely an ecumenical function, not an evangelistic—as traditionally defined—one. I see no reason why boards for Christian unity and boards for world witness should not be combined.

Other traditional, denominationally based functions remain to be considered. Most, if not all, mainline denominations maintain a string of liberal arts colleges and universities that at one time were the backbone of both academics and churchmanship. I attended such a school, whose motto read, "Christian Education—the Hope of the World." Half a century ago significant numbers of graduating high school students chose a college because it belonged to their denomination. The administration and faculty, as well as the student body, operated as an extension of the work of the larger church.

While the number of these church colleges multiplied, their relation to the church faded dramatically. In my denomination there were—and still are—five institutions of higher education within my state, Missouri. But their current relationship to the denomination, or its congregations, is hazy at best. Since significant amounts of money for higher education now come directly or indirectly from government sources, church-state issues are increasingly troublesome.

It may be that maintaining these schools as church related is more a matter of sentiment than anything else. It is difficult to see how denominational structures that attempt to coordinate the work of these schools are any longer justified. It is even more difficult to see how they can be financed.

This leaves two other functions currently being performed at the denominational level. One has to do with the training of ministers. To that we will return shortly. The other has to do with certain functions that are at the same time pastoral and administrative. Most denominations have someone who is the president of the church, even though that title varies from group to group. When we say person, we really mean office, and that means staff—lots of staff—lots of very expensive staff. My denomination has one executive officer whose title is "General Minister and President." As President this person is the chief operating officer of the corporation. As General Minister he is the chief pastor and theologian. It is an impossible job. The time may be at hand when all the administrative functions currently being performed by this person should be placed in a separate portfolio. All the administrative tasks, including those listed on page 144 might well be turned over to an office headed by the best business head the church can find. This would most likely be a lay position. He or she would be responsible for running the business. This would allow the head of the church to be pastor and theologian—General Minister.

Every local pastor has been challenged by well-meaning layfolk with the declaration: "The church should operate more like a business." I believe the church should operate more like a church! It is rooted in faith, not in profits. It looks at theological authenticity as the measure of its success, not the bottom line. Its leader needs to be clear about goals, lest the church become just another American business, committed to making all the charts go up. The head of the church, therefore, must be its clearest, most articulate theological voice.

Protecting Against the Tyranny of the Local

Whatever the mainline church looks like down the road, its life will primarily be focused in the work of the congregation. The denomination beyond the congregation will exist primarily to support the work of its local units—act as agent to assist the whole church in doing what the congregation cannot. But the power and program of general units will be greatly reduced, as will their budgets and control over how the resources of the whole church are to be allocated. Major decisions and practically all programming will originate and be executed at the level closest to the people. Denominations will not go out of business, but the scope of their work and their visibility will be much more circumscribed. Some of what they have traditionally done will be assigned to ecumenical bodies. We will no longer have the luxury of a score of mainline communions duplicating what can and should be done in concert. The role of ecumenical bodies will be discussed in Chapter Eleven.

One major caveat must be stated in light of the current fascination with the centrality of the congregation. There is inevitably a tyranny that comes with too heavy a reliance on the local, particularly when it involves the articulation of the faith. This has become even truer as congregations have been less centers of theological reflection and inquiry, and more community-based social groups. As local churches have been increasingly diluted with those from whom little commitment and less biblical knowledge is required, a more prejudicial understanding of faith has evolved, growing out of the ethos of the culture. The task of the whole church must be to act as a lighthouse and buffer against local theological tyrannies.

In denomination after denomination the observable phenomenon has been the same. It is almost always true that when the denomination assembles to do its work, what is said and decided does not mirror what would happen if the members of each congregation voted and the results simply tabulated. Congregations one at a time tend to be far more conservative in their social outlook than either their general units or their national conventions. In some eras the danger lies in the tyranny of a hierarchy. That is not the problem of the mainline church today. Our difficulty lies in the opposite direction. We are in danger of being controlled by people who take their cues from the prevailing culture, not from their faith. Today that means the invasion of faith by a conservative political agenda.

Since biblical texts and religious perspectives can be found to prove almost everything, we find what appears to be a Christian justification for some very curious secular presuppositions. "Christians" often take the reactionary agenda of the society around them and find religious reasons to believe it. The more tightly drawn the local ethos, the further these secular propositions clothed in religious language are from the faith of the church at large.

An assembly of the leaders of the church may support the control of handguns, or the escalation of nuclear disarmament, or the dignity of farmworkers, or the securing of civil rights for the pariahs in society. But if congregations were to vote one at a time on any of these issues, chances are the result would be far different. A generation ago every major mainline denomination took a clear position on civil rights. That issue considered by the lay leaders of congregations throughout the American South would have elicited a very different result. Many congregations came kicking and screaming to the conclusion that segregation was contrary to the nature of God's reign, and therefore had no place either in the church or in the world. Even today in some isolated places a vote of the church board, let alone the congregation, would still affirm the right of a church or a business to operate on the theory that the races ought to be kept separated.

The only way to overcome local prejudices is for the church beyond the congregation to be clear about the intent of the gospel, and to say so on behalf of the whole church. The case must be made by those best prepared theologically to articulate the implications of the faith, and that is why the president of the denomination needs to be the finest theological mind available.

The problem is not new in our era. It is currently complicated by a laity that is less inclined to be biblically or theologically reflective. It is doubtful that a majority of mainline congregations, voting one at a time, would have supported the end of slavery, the franchising of women, the support of the rights of labor, the abolition of capital punishment, or the termination of the Vietnam war. And yet, when the churches met in assemblies, they were increasingly clear about every one of those issues. The reason is that the percentage of attending ministers—the local churches' theologians—biblically able laypeople, seminary professors, and other leaders tend to be far greater than one would find in the typical congregation.

These days practically every denomination has within its ranks an organized group whose perspective is significantly more conservative than is the whole church or its leaders. One lament coming from these groups is that denominational officials, and the assemblies of the whole church, do not reflect what folks in the pews are thinking. Seminary professors in particular are said to be out of touch with the laity. What is loudly called for by these quasi-fundamentalists is a change in format so that the denomination, when assembled, more accurately reflects what the people it represents are really saying.

But are the conventions and the leaders of the church called to represent their constituencies? To what extent does the whole church reflect the views of its members—that is, embody a pure democracy—and to what extent does it entrust those called to lead it to articulate what they understand to be the will of God? Obviously the right of individual conscience cannot be dismissed. But that is far different than suggesting the gospel is understood to be what any person or social group says it is. Neither Martin Luther nor Martin Luther King, Jr., spoke after counting hands.

One result of this hiatus between many members of the laity and the position of the whole church assembled has been increasingly popular campaigns to eliminate denominational advocacy on social issues. This would include both resolutions before assemblies of the church and positions taken by the national units and agencies. One denominational president reported that wherever he had gone there was general enthusiastic support within the church to eliminate from its assembly agendas up or down votes on those issues on which there was not general agreement among the congregations. While there were other voices within the structure of the denomination that resisted the retreat, in this and other mainline bodies there has been an increasing hesitancy to offend the conservatives.

If fundamentalism continues to exercise increasing power among mainline congregations, and denominations are finally captured by it, the day may arrive when the only option for those committed to an authentic future is to withdraw. That is what is currently happening among many Southern Baptists who can no longer sit quietly while witch hunts go on in seminaries, and positions articulated that no thinking Christian can countenance.

There are strident voices that hold that unless denominational officials yield to the reactionary voices within their midst, they may end up as leaders without followers. There is considerable evidence that an increasing number of conservative congregations are distancing themselves from their denominations. If these prophets of doom are correct, it is widely assumed that either denominational leaders must learn to operate within a conservative environment, or they will end up isolated, out of touch with constituencies shrunk to the point of no return. The alternative is for denominational leaders to become teachers of faith once more, forsaking their assumed roles as executives of religious institutions.

Again it is clear that the difficulty lies in the general theological malaise that has infected congregations. The more local churches have become community social units committed to food, fun, and fellowship for those of all ages and interests, the more the inclination has been to pretend the last two hundred years of biblical scholarship never occurred. Church members then tend to take their views of the world from secular structures that engulf them. And in our era that means a strident conservatism. The other popular option is to retreat into an radical religious sectarianism, which sees itself as over against the secular society, but does so by embracing biblical literalism and the use of a handful of proof texts.

A significant number of ministers have confided to me that they dare not raise controversial issues before their congregations. Most of their members assume that the Bible is literally, scientifically, and historically accurate. One minister told me he was startled when he realized that most of his communicants now hold to a six-day creation six thousand years ago, and an ark into which Noah crowded several hundreds of thousands of animal species. While this minister was startled at the discovery, he had never posed any other option! He didn't realize that was his job.

It is doubtful that this trend can or will be quickly reversed. The law of social inertia means that tomorrow will probably be fundamentally like today. Social change occasionally comes by revolution, but most often the process is evolutionary. It will take a new generation of ministers who see themselves as theologians in residence, not as program directors.

In the meantime, denominational leaders will remain in an impossible position. The change must first come from renewed congregations, and that will not happen short of a new generation of parish ministers willing to break through the typical congregational structure and mind-set.

The Middle Judicatory

Every denomination has situated between the general or national level of the church and the congregation a unit variously called a conference, district, diocese, presbytery, or region. Sometime ago these bodies became known as judicatories, an artless and unfortunate term. In some churches they were once the locus of the ecclesiastical courts, thus the title. While a change in name does not necessarily entail a change in function, some better, more theologically consistent term than judicatory needs to be developed. We will suggest one at the end of this section.

While these ecclesial units have been hard-pressed to define their functions within the life of the whole church, they have tended to grow like topsy. If in most denominations the general church formerly determined how much money coming from congregations was to be assigned to various units and agencies, increasingly these middle structures have demanded a greater and greater share of the revenues, and have found ways to intercept the congregations' outreach dollars before they were passed farther up the line. In some bodies there continues a vigorous struggle between these middle units and the national church. The issue is, as always, power; and power, as always, means the control of budgets. Since I take the political process seriously, for many years I have refused to serve on any body, in either the church or in the community, which was called "advisory." The structures that make the difference are those having the authority to decide how the money is to be spent and who is going to spend it.

Even while their growth has been phenomenal, among these extra-congregational bodies the demand for an increased share of the financial pie has been unabated. It was obvious to mid-range ecclesiastical officials and their boards that all the money—beyond endowments—ultimately came from their congregations. As the economic capacity of congregations continued to shrink, the obvious answer paralleled that produced by the denominational structures above them: assist congregations to become dynamic faith communities. That, or similar language, has become a code for church growth. Proposed solutions did not speak so much of making hard decisions about how a diminished pie was to be divided, but how the size of the pie might be increased. If the problem was fervently addressed, it was not solved. Despite their efforts, pies baked by congregations have continued to grow smaller.

Regional bodies tend to be centered on program development, not on theological reflection. On the one hand, they have become vehicles for the promotion of denominational programs. On the other hand, they have attempted to replicate within their geographic areas programs most effectively done by congregations.

As resources continue to wither, judicatories will be faced with declining prospects and must deal with significant cuts in both programs and staff. Either intelligent church members will decide what programs at various levels need to be suspended, or history will make those decisions on the basis of political power struggles. In some denominations the fight has already gotten nasty—the regional bodies organized against their national counterparts. Since they are closer to the money, and the congregations that produce it, regions tend to have the strategic advantage. It is the regions that provide camps and conferences for young people, develop leadership training events for teachers and other leaders within congregations, and are much more hesitant to take controversial positions that might alienate the conservatives in local churches.

Suggestions have begun to surface that would eventually eliminate these middle units. While political realities legislate against any such move, it is obvious their roles and their financial resources will continue to suffer. Wisdom means that decisions about these retrenchments will be made ahead of time and intelligently, not under the immediate duress of deficits. It is too late to decide on the proper compass heading when all your energy is being used in bailing out a sinking ship.

What might be the essential functions of these middle units during a period of captivity, and how can more limited definitions be implemented? First, it must be asked which of these essential functions cannot be effectively performed by national bodies, and are also beyond the capacity of congregations. A careful analysis reveals only four.

First, certain limited programmatic functions are clearly regional in nature. Few congregations can build and maintain a conference and retreat center. While in some areas these facilities need to be rented, or jointly held by several denominations, in other locations they can be self-sufficient. There are enough secular bodies willing to pay good rental fees for first-rate facilities to make them economically viable.

Second, there are certain leadership training events that may best be conducted at the regional level. In Chapter Five we suggested that no teachers be turned loose on students until they have been credentialed at some level, or served under a senior teacher who has been. It may be that the region is the appropriate training, if not authorizing, body.

Third, a regional officer variously known at bishop, regional or conference minister, or simply secretary is necessary to act as the pastor to pastors, and also as the person responsible for the orderly call or appointment of pastors to congregations.

Ask any parish minister and you will hear that his or her denomination's method of linking churches and pastors is terrible. There may be no good systems. And yet, each church somehow will end up with its pastor, or share one with a neighboring congregation, or do without. In most mainline churches the congregation will have a large share in the final say, even if it happens discreetly as seems to be the case among United Methodists.

Given the complexities of ministerial placement, and the opportunity for getting the wrong person in the wrong pulpit, exercising some oversight is a must for the church beyond the congregation. It is the conference or synod that may be best positioned to consult with and assist congregations in pastoral transition—and to do the same for ministers seeking to relocate. For our purposes we need not define how the system might best work, only that it will ultimately rely on support from the larger church. The regional body is probably also best positioned to process ordinations and determine ministerial standing. Save us from ministers who are law to themselves and responsible to nobody, and from congregations that see themselves as single-church denominations, or who believe they are independent of the whole body.

Someone outside the congregation, but not that far away geographically, is essential in helping congregations and ministers when there is trouble. Left to their own devices, otherwise solid churches have been torn to shreds by ministers who have lost their way. I have also listened to scores of ministers, of all ages, as they have shared their suffering and heartache at the hands of brutal congregations, or more likely a handful of congregants who were out to get them. Sometimes the difficulty has been over social witness or doctrine. Sometimes it has been over ministerial malfeasance or sloth. When the minister is right, he or she needs to be defended by someone who is in a position of trust and authority. When the minister is wrong, discipline is in order, and that comes best from a representative of the whole church.

There are even occasions when the regional officer might well be given the authority to remove the minister and/or dissolve the local session or board. While this is a difficulty for free churches, given the emergency that applies during the present captivity, it could be thought of as akin to martial law.

Some official body beyond the local church must take responsibility when congregations have completed their effective work and need to be closed or merged. This is most always a painful situation that deserves to be treated with respect and dignity. If, on the other hand, the opportunity arises for the planting of a new church, the oversight of a region is also important.

The fourth, and central task, of an ecclesiastical office beyond the congregation is theological. The person heading this unit must be a theologian as well as a pastor. He or she is the pastor to pastors and the teachers of these theologians in residence. Even though we have insisted on the centrality of the teaching task of the local minister, we do not disparage administration. In the congregation that is the job of the laity, but certainly some administrative skills ought to be in place for those who work at the wider level. The problem seems to be that persons in these middle judicatory positions are often administratively adequate, but theologically inept. If congregations during this captivity, are to become smaller, more highly committed bodies of the faithful, then master teachers need to be available. That means the local pastor must be supported at the regional level, and the obvious person to fill that role is the conference minister.

During this discussion we have varied the designations we have used because they vary from denomination to denomination. If we are looking for one commonly agreed upon title for the individual assuming the leadership of this extra-congregational unit no matter what it is called, perhaps the biblical word "bishop" is most appropriate. While that term carries negative connotations in a number of mainline churches, historically it strikes the right note. The bishop has traditionally been the keeper and teacher of the faith. The problem has arisen when bishops become the chief manipulators in church politics, on one hand, and administrators on the other. While each denomination will select its own names for officers and units, the terms "bishop" and "region" strike me as the best ways to identify the officers and the units between the congregation and the denomination at large.

The Continued Renewal of the Theological Seminary

More than all other church-related institutions, seminaries have been profoundly aware of and shaped by the captivity of the mainline church. And yet over the past generation they have produced a sturdy cadre of men and women who have been at a loss as to how to grapple with the changing role of the congregations they have been trained to serve.

In the early 1970s, I was the entire homiletics and liturgical faculty at a leading seminary of one of the major mainline denominations—and I was a part-time, adjunct, stop gap. During those years most ministerial students held the parish in considerable disdain. When they graduated these students were going to do anything other than become pastors of local churches. They believed that congregation were irrelevant and out of touch. These bright, and for the most part radical young people, were going into specialized ministries with political implications. They were out to revolutionize the world. Many had come to school via the civil rights and anti-Vietnam War movements.

Upon graduation, however, they discovered that opportunities to earn a living in ways they had imagined were almost nonexistent. Many of these graduates rejected ordination, and found themselves in a variety of secular jobs, from insurance to social work.

Many of those who did remain in the church, having taken jobs in the very parishes they had previously disdained, found exactly what they had predicted, and have all too often spent their careers planning for retirement.

A significant number realized that any hope of radicalizing the congregations they were called to serve was futile, and looked once more for alternate forms of ministry where they had some hope of making a difference. They found a plethora of clinically based pastoral care training centers, primarily in hospitals, or they became enamored with pietistic spiritual disciplines or church growth techniques.

It was this last group of the ordained who often settled for being programmers, marketers, and social directors. A solid number, still looking for vocational stability and a way to deeper meaning, returned to the seminary in order to obtain one of the ubiquitous doctor of ministry degrees, which helped not a few academic institutions swell general enrollments. Many of the major academic projects of these returning students turned out to focus on church growth. Seminaries were slow to distinguish that discipline from evangelism, and even established departments and chairs of church growth, assuming that the two concerns were identical. Churches far and wide, however, benefited from the sharpening of the intellectual tools of ministers who often experienced remarkable personal growth. Since the inception of doctor of ministry programs, seminaries have had to rethink the nature of these degrees.

Coincidental with the development of the D.Min., many ministers began to long for a new sense of status in their communities. Standing gained from being the local "person" or "parson" had long since passed. They were no longer the only educated persons in town. Many longed to be seen along with doctors, dentists, lawyers, architects, and college professors as members of the professional elite. A spate of professional organizations for clergy began to appear. While part of their agendas had to do with the ill-treatment ministers often received at the hands of occasionally abrasive congregations, it became too easy to focus on new ways to achieve privilege and acclamation. As the captivity of mainline churches became more severe, the hunger for acceptance grew, and the distance from the goals of an authentic church began to be more obvious. When professional salaries did not follow, the edge was taken off the image. The result was often what came to be known as ministerial burnout. The real problems were often disillusionment and boredom.

To the extent seminaries were distanced from these dynamics, they continued to produce ministers unable to cope with the rapidly emerging issues before the congregations they were called to serve. This was particularly true in the more academically reputable divinity schools, where many faculty members were almost totally out of touch with the church. These were often graduate centers of religious studies, which along the way had developed professional degrees for those who wanted some day to be engaged in the practice of ministry. Their main task, however, was to train Ph.D.s, who would become the professors in other graduate schools and in seminaries. The further removed from the life of the parish and its dynamics, the greater the problems down in the trenches when students hit the parish beaches.

Other schools, more closely related to the church, whose faculty members tended to be deeply involved in local congregations, were quicker to see the development of the problem facing mainline institutions, and began, albeit slowly, to respond to the new reality. Perhaps no seminary primarily engaged in the training of parish ministers ought to accept faculty members not committed to and active in the church.

Seminaries were faced with two other challenges, both having to do with the nature of the students they were able to recruit. First was the influx of secon-career enrollees, who in middle years were seeking a vocation with more meaning than their former jobs had provided. While a few of these ministerial recruits came from other professions, a significant number had held jobs that had not demanded high levels of academic sophistication. Placing these graduates, whose average age was over forty, was not always easy. Many more were given degrees than finally found their way into pulpits, and many who did were ill prepared to take the church in new directions, and settled for attempting to emulate the parishes in which they had grown up. The dedication of these second-career ministers was often exemplary. Their maturity proved beneficial. Their academic and theological skills were often limited.

Consider the following:

In 1991 the average age of students in theological seminaries of five mainline churches was:

Episcopal Church	40.3
The United Church of Christ	40.1

The United Methodist Church	38.0
The Presbyterian Church	36.5
The Christian Church (D of C)	34.5

Seminaries were simultaneously faced with an increasing number of women of all ages, seeking entrance into the ministerial ranks. The time came in many seminaries when the ratio of men to women was one to one.

> Consider the following: In 1962 seminary students in all graduate schools were 91.3 percent male, 8.7 percent female. By 1991 males formed 68 percent of student bodies and females 32 percent.

But those statistics include churches that do not accept women students.

Among the five mainline churches referred to above the following figures define the percentage of women in the student bodies:

The Episcopal Church	40.3
The United Church of Christ	40.1
The United Methodist Church	38.0
The Presbyterian Church	36.5
The Christian Church (D of C)	34.5

More recent studies would indicate that the trend is still on the increase.

Early on it was widely believed that congregations would not accept women as pastors. Indeed, women had a difficult time attracting calls, and often the calls they did get were to the least promising positions. As time went on, however, it began to dawn on congregations that many of these women brought an amazing set of skills with them, and slowly the clerical glass ceiling began to crack.

Women often turned out to be among the most effective practitioners, pastorally and theologically. In the community where I last served, the most dynamic and able younger pastors were two women, one Presbyterian and the other United Methodist. As neighboring congregations observed their effectiveness, gender-based prejudices were gradually eroded.

Seminaries, which had long been dominated by males, were forced to deal with a new set of realities beginning with the curriculum.

Probably more than any other factor, the feminization of seminaries, which meant the gradual feminization of congregations, has offered the church, as well as its training institutions, a fresh set of challenges and a new sense of hope, as well as new insights into the forgotten feminine aspects of faith. Women in ministry is no longer a problem in the mainline church. It is, in fact, one of the great hopes.

Maintaining the Unity of the Church

The church has existed from generation to generation on the basis of its inherent oneness. No part of the church can exist alone or independent of every other part. This need is particularly important during periods of stress and captivity. While the functions must necessarily change, the need for officers and units beyond the congregation will continue to be essential. Even if much of what denominations now do in both their national and regional manifestations is probably passé and unfundable, they cannot be allowed to die. We must continue to rely on each other.

Beyond denominational structures there is an even larger matter that involves the unity of the church. To that ecumenical concern we now turn.

Questions for Reflection and Discussion

1. Is your denomination as healthy as it was a generation ago? How do you evaluate the signs of health or disease within the larger church?

2. What changes do you currently note in mainline denominations and their intermediate units—often called "judicatories"?

3. How is your congregation dependent on the denomination? What are the ways you operate without reference to the church beyond your community?

4. Are there aggressive congregations in your community that seem to have no denominational ties? What are the benefits and the liabilities of such arrangements—or lack of them?

5. What case can be made for the autonomy of any facet of church life? Can a congregation really be a "law to itself"?

6. What things can be done only cooperatively? What things can be best done only at the congregational level?

7. Can you recite instances where congregations have been dominated by persons who use the church to meet their own needs for control?

8. What happens in your congregation when the denomination takes a position on a controversial issue, and members of your congregation raise strong objections? For instance, the denomination may call the government to control the proliferation of handguns, and there are powerful members of the congregation who belong to the National Rifle Association.

9. Does your pastor have a pastor from the denomination? What is the role of the area judicatory leader—bishop, regional minister, conference executive, district superintendent? How does the regional body, whatever its name, function in relationship to your congregation?

10. Are there any changes in society or church life that call for a rethinking of the role of the regional church?

11. "Bishops" have historically been teachers of the faith. In recent years they have become more administrators than theologians. Can this trend be reversed—or should it be?

12. How is the proliferation in the seminaries of older second-career persons and women bound to affect your denomination and its congregations? Is your congregation ready to accept pastoral leadership from other than a middle-aged male? What would your congregation have to do to prepare for such an opportunity?

11 | Ecumenism and a Church in Exile

We turn to a topic that has disturbed and weakened the church almost from the beginning. The three great scandals of Christendom have been (1) its too-easy accommodation to national, ethnic, racial, and social majorities so that it excluded, warred against, persecuted, and even killed off great numbers of God's children; (2) its failure to evidence the nature of God's reign of peace and justice; and (3) its lack of unity. We now consider how this third issue, the fragmentation of the church, seriously complicates the present captivity.

The Sin of Our Divisions

A few years ago I spent a sabbatical in Greece. I went there with a specific academic project in mind. I wanted to find out how the second-generation church in Corinth dealt with the social issues discussed in Paul's first letter. Was that body of Christians able to overcome the divisions Paul had noted, and make a unified witness? I realized solid documentation might be difficult to find, but I would not have been the first person to attempt the reconstruction of an entire dinosaur from the fragment of a jawbone. After considerable digging, I came to a startling conclusion. The church that Paul founded probably did not survive! Its divisions did it in. The introduction of Christianity into that part of the world dates from the work of later missionaries and other travelers who came from Rome, not from Judea.

Here was a fragile church under siege. The culture was hostile. Corinth was a profoundly secular city. While religious temples and artifacts abounded, they were fundamentally the products of what we today would call civil religion. If the fledgling Christian community that Paul brought into being was pressed on one side by a virulent secularism, it was pressed on the other side by charismatics and fundamentalists within its own ranks. The charismatics were probably represented by the followers of Apollo. These were the speakers in the tongues of angels. The fundamentalists were rigid Messianists, who called themselves after Christ, or they were from the party of Cephas, who represented the persistent Jewish orthodoxy of the Judean church.

Since that day, division within the church has been a horrid evil. If the fragmentation of the Christian community is unhappy news in any era, how much more devastating is the problem for a community in captivity! The unity of the church is, therefore, essential to its survival. Consider the complications that division portends in a post-ecumenical age.

The Decline of Ecumenism

A generation or two ago, the ecumenical spirit was in high gear among mainline denominations. Councils of churches in almost every sizable community were thriving, with their own staffs, programs, and comity commissions that helped the various denominations plant new congregations out of each other's way. The National Council of Churches had reached maturity, and was widely heralded as the voice of Protestantism. The World Council was increasingly seen as inaugurating a new global ecumenical age. The dialogue between Catholics and Protestants, following the lead of Pope John XXIII, was highlighted by living room discussion groups all across North America. In Australia, Canada, India, and elsewhere, mergers produced united churches. The Consultation on Church Union had taken off with a half-dozen denominations determined to create one body.

Now, three or four decades later, the landscape is littered with the debris of diminished hopes and failed dreams. Local councils are practically nonexistent. The National Council of Churches faces crisis after crisis, and every effort to restructure it only exacerbates its problems. The World Council, and movements for church union in the Third World, are still strong, although in Africa, Asia, and Latin America charismatics and fundamentalists are now far more aggressive and increasingly popular among the poor. Pope John XXIII and his open spirit are long gone. COCU is a curious shadow, at least at the grassroots, supported by a few passionate ecumenists within the participating denominations, and ignored by practically everyone else.

Consider the level of ecumenical interest one currently finds in mainline congregations. To say that no one is attentive may be an overstatement. But I would be hard-pressed to name a congregation where Christian unity or the Consultation on Church Union is presently seen as vital to the life of the community. In the progressive congregation I last served, one could hold a well-publicized meeting on these subjects in a phone booth. Now and then one hears about a joint effort to plant a new church, or about the merger of congregations of like-minded denominations, but not often.

At the moment when we most need each other, we seem to be most distant. It is not that theological issues divide us. The World Council of Churches' statement on *Baptism, Eucharist, and Ministry* demonstrated an amazing level of theological agreement throughout the mainline community, as well as among Roman Catholics and the Orthodox.

There are reasons for the demise of the concern for Christian unity. In churches where theological matters are not widely discussed or held to be of overriding importance, the issue is rarely even raised. When the church is a social system, only economic pressures would justify such conversations. People tend to join churches based on location, convenience, programs offered, and the compatibility of those with whom one might share a pew, and not matters of doctrine. Since formal conversations about unity are almost universally based in discussions of faith and religious practice, there is now little ground for debate, discussion, and common understanding. Working through the theological knots that have divided the church is irrelevant in congregations where theology is not at the heart of things.

At the other end of the spectrum—life and work as opposed to faith and order—there is already a commonality of purpose and mission. Few mainline churches would consider engaging in operating a food kitchen for the poor, or a housing project, or a shelter for the homeless, without consulting with other like-minded congregations in the community. If at one time local councils of churches were necessary to provide forums for common action, these days joint projects are entered into much more informally. A few ministers or members of the laity get together at lunch, plan a project, and then see to its execution. In other communities this sort of activity is coordinated by a quasi-secular social service body, which operates with both church and tax dollars. Joint worship services on Thanksgiving and during Holy Week are planned in conversations over the ecclesial back fence.

"Walking Together"

A few years ago, not only were a solid collection of mainline denominations discussing merger, but other bilateral negotiations were taking place aimed at reducing the number of competing denominations in the United States. The United Church of Christ and the Christian Church (Disciples of Christ) were planning to form a new combined body. As the ecumenical fervor seemed to erode, the nature of these discussions and the work of the Consultation on Church Union dramatically changed. COCU enthusiasts protested that they never had intended to create a super church, but rather to find common ways of work and worship so that intercommunion, the mutual recognition of ministers, and the acknowledgment of the legitimacy of each other's members were possible. Walking together, not merger, became the dominant theme. However, that position was clearly a retreat from the original Blake-Pike proposal, which called for a united church. The planning body, COCU, had the term "union" built into its name.

Now hopes for even a joint walk have dimmed. It is not that there seems to be any serious objection or unsolvable doctrinal matters, but that few seem to care. The same is true of the bilateral conversations. The Disciples and the United Church of Christ are increasingly wary of each other, and most of their negotiations have been reduced to polite interchanges. Interestingly, the two overseas mission boards seem committed to a merger no matter what the denominations at-large do or refuse to do. Having once talked seriously about marriage, these two bodies now have settled for a cordial platonic relationship.

While COCU might once have produced a dynamic united church, that opportunity now appears to be on the back side of history. There are moments when enormous strides forward are possible—tides in the affairs of churches. Taken at their flood they lead on to unity, but when the tide begins to ebb, the opportunity is gone, if not forever, at least for some time. And the sands along the vacant seacoast show little more than the repositioning of some dunes, significant to few beside ecclesiastic archeologists.

If, however, the effectiveness of denominations as we have known them is over, or at least subject to enormous change, it is doubtful that the merger of these dated ecclesial systems would make much sense. Some further exploration of the walking together theme may be the most productive avenue during this period of captivity. There are things we can do jointly without an attempt to fit overly large bureaucratic structures into a single framework. In fact, the enormous effort it would take to bring that off might be a misuse of energy in an era when the resources of the mainline churches are urgently needed elsewhere. And as valuable as the National Council of Churches has been, keeping it afloat may use up energy that is critical to the performance of other functions.

It is possible to affirm our oneness without the mechanical encumbrances involved in mergers. We can recognize each other's sacraments, ministry, and members without having to merge structures. There can be de facto agreements about how we send personnel overseas and how we deal with the media at home. But to consolidate pension boards and administrative offices may be futile, unwieldy, and unnecessary.

Facing the New Divisions

Despite the obvious institutional divisions that have fractured the life of each of the mainline communions, at heart each senses that the others are part of Christ's body, and therefore, for all intents and purposes, they are already united. There is now a growing unity of the spirit in the bond of peace. Mainliners rarely consider each other to be outside the faith. The differences are said to be matters of opinion, not matters of essence. The fact that organizational unity eludes us may not be of consequence during these years of our captivity. We may still be divided in matters of structure, but we may be already united in those things that really count in the proclamation and demonstration of the coming reign of God.

The substantial divisions among Protestants in our day cut across denominational lines and penetrate every one of our traditional communions. To put it bluntly, the members of every congregation I have served know that they have more in common with other Presbyterians in our community, or United Methodists, Evangelical Lutherans, those of the United Church of Christ or folks from the nearby Episcopal Church than they have with some congregations of their own denomination.

The narrowly defined antagonists, who have been a growing force throughout mainline religion, also find compatible colleagues in similar groups in other denominations. The Biblical Witness Fellowship of the United Church of Christ and Disciples Renewal of The Christian Church (Disciples of Christ) have much more in common than they have with the majorities in their own communions. It is an anomaly that the two denominations have been in merger conversations for years. Left to their own, the liberals in each group and the conservatives in each group can independently pursue common goals and "walk together." The conservatives in each camp, however, believe the liberals in both camps to be heretics, while the liberals in both camps believe the conservatives to be uncharitable and divisive.

Leaders in mainline denominations may be so caught up in trying to keep peace within their own bodies, that there is little capacity left for the wider ecumenical challenges. Such are the issues confronting a church whose fragmentation has reinforced its own captivity and contributed to its own weakness.

I recently was an unofficial observer at the national meeting of an Australian denomination in which the internal division was both obvious and energy draining. The week was spent debating two issues: whether congregations should allowed to use candles and oil in their baptismal rites, and whether the word "honor" should be included in the marriage vows for brides but not for grooms. Underneath these seemingly arcane disputes was the divisive core issue: liberal vs. conservative, or as they would tend to put it: Anglo-Catholic vs. Evangelicals. That division cuts differently than the American version, but the impact is the same. The collection of empty or nearly empty parish churches represented by the two hundred officials in the assembly testified to how out of touch much of the mainline church is. The hopeful aspect of the weeklong meeting was that this body was talking about theology, not just about marketing. Nevertheless, given the two matters that dominated the sessions, officers commanding troops dug in on the front lines do not have the luxury of debating the color of their dress uniforms.

Prospects for agreement beyond life and work are dismal in the current ecclesial environment. For the time being, perhaps the best we can hope for is that at the denominational level, leaders can set aside their doctrinal disputes and act together in ways that may be salvific for the society at large. Fundamentalists within the mainline denominations will settle for nothing less than their own version of doctrinal purity. If we wait until the issues they want to raise are settled, we will have waited too long.

Ecumenicity at Grass Roots

During the present captivity, the success of our ecumenical bodies will be severely limited. Let us hope that the National Council of Churches survives its current struggles, and is reincarnated in some vital form. The future of the World Council seems more certain, although it too will be limited in its witness. At best it can keep Protestants and Orthodox within hearing distance, and also maintain a dignified forum for encounters with Roman Catholics. It can also serve to encourage churches in the Third World to persist in walking together. Having come to terms with a more realistic agenda, COCU may produce limited results. Most local councils will not survive, although the multifaceted social service agencies they have spawned will last as long as dollars flow from a variety of governmental programs. It is unlikely that very many of them could make it if congregations were the only economic support.

If there is to be any substantial hope for the unity of the church, it will probably come from small groups of committed people who think and work together in local communities. Much of this activity will be subject to economic pressures. Money drives many things—

good and ill. So does its lack. There are groups of Christians who will find each other because they cannot afford to do anything else.

The more a congregation becomes a center for theological reflection, the more likely it will favor combining its efforts with other like-minded congregations in the community. The more a congregation is a "birds of a feather" social group, the more likely it will be to sit in its dark and decaying building until the last member expires and some ecclesiastical mortician has to come in and turn off the lights. It is sad beyond measure to witness a string of downtown churches continue to decline until none of them has the strength left to do anything but provide religious nursing home care for those who are left.

In denominations where somebody beyond the congregation can speak with authority, there may be new opportunities to merge congregations of the same brand. Even so, the merger of two desperately weak congregations does not necessary make for one strong one. Chances are that the dying will carry the same mind-set into the merger they developed during their years of decline. The time to join forces, either within the same denomination or across denominational lines, is when there is enough vitality left to make something of the merger.

Some of the strongest congregations—not largest, but strongest—can be found among theologically literate groups of people who come together because they realize that by the will and intention of Christ, they belong together. In urban areas such mergers often provide the opportunity for significant cross-cultural and interracial relationships. Those who cooperate out of a faith commitment will find in each other partners and fellow pilgrims. Those for whom the church is only their social unit, probably will not.

Throughout this book we have argued that the main task of the minister is to be the theologian in residence. Three or four ministers—or only two—who have redefined their roles may discover that the most effective teaching will cross congregational and denominational lines.

The model may be seminaries in the same city, which have developed joint faculties, or at least classes open to those in each of the institutions. In Melbourne, Australia, the Baptists and the Churches of Christ have joined to form the Evangelical Theological Association, which sees itself as having one faculty and class schedule on two campuses. If educational institutions can do it, how much simpler for a brace of like-minded but theologically diverse congregations to engage in a joint effort to develop biblically literate, theologically alert communities of faith.

We know how to cooperate across all kinds of denominational lines. We do it all the time. Informal cross-congregational groups have established thousands of programs for the relief of hunger, as well as clothing centers and housing units for low-income or elderly citizens. We have been advocates for the poor and taken up concerted programs on behalf of the pariahs in our midst. Churches were at the heart of the struggle for human rights. We have been central to the pleas for peace and disarmament. No movement or organization for the humanization of our culture would have gotten to first base without the support, personnel, funds, ideological clout and discipline of mainline churches operating in concert. Now our task is to provide the biblical and theological underpinnings for a new day. And that work will be best done together.

If God is the God of history, not just of nature, then history is the judgment of God. We reap the fruit of the seed we have sown. Jeremiah may not have gotten it right. The children's teeth are often set on edge by the sour grapes the parents have eaten. Our stubborn sectarianism, in our generation without even solid theological justification, may have lasted so long and become so entrenched that the potter will refuse to make from the sodden clay vessels suitable for the work to be done. We may be stuck with God, but God is not stuck with us. What we do affects God. That is what it means when we affirm that God is the God of history. God is always adjusting the pattern in response to events. That is what the cross tells us. Indeed, that is what every page of the scriptural tradition affirms.

And yet there is a grace in the work and will of God that is greater than all our sins, and even in the face of our divisions and our divisiveness, there may yet come vessels of beauty. At least we must live with that hope, or what in life and faith is worth the effort? In the meantime, mending what we can of a badly bruised and torn body must stay near the top of the agenda of the mainline church.

Questions for Reflection and Discussion

1. A generation ago most mainline denominations and their congregations evidenced a profound concern for the unity of the church. Ecumenism was a major item on the agenda. If a passion for the unity of the church has cooled, what has been the cause, and what are the results?

2. Is there an active Council of Churches in your community? If there was at one time, but not now, what happened to it? Are there new interchurch or interfaith programs that have replaced it?

3. Describe your involvement in and attitude about the National and the World Councils of Churches.

4. How has *Baptism, Eucharist, and Ministry* been used in your congregation and among the churches of your community?

5. Is your denomination a member of the Consultation on Church Union? If so, how does membership influence life in your congregation?

6. New divisions have occurred within most mainline churches. Many evangelicals feel less and less at home and are now forming what appear to be new denominations. How has this affected life in the parent body?

7. Have there been mergers among congregations in your community, or are there ways in which new forms of cooperative ministries are taking place?

12 | "Love the Church!"

Some time back I had the occasion to preside at an ordination service for a young man who had been raised in our congregation. From his earliest years Greg was a singularly bright, sensitive, and committed young man. As a freshman in high school he heard how the Nestle company was merchandising canned milk to mothers in the Third World, after having convinced them that they should not nurse their offspring. He was irate. It so happened that the school's major student fund-raiser that year was the sale of candy bars produced by the company in question. Greg mounted a one-person campaign, which resulted in the cancellation of the candy contract. Not everyone was pleased. Worthwhile enterprises that would have benefited from the candy sale did not receive funding. Greg was called a do-gooder and a communist. And yet, he had inspired a respect for poor women around the world. At least there was one teenager in town who commanded the attention of a community by raising an ethical issue of some importance—even at personal risk.

Over the next several years Greg's social conscience was further sharpened, and he became active in the anti-nuclear movement in the community, as well as in the effort to unveil the deception he believed the United States was practicing in Latin America.

While at college he led a campaign, which involved civil disobedience, to have his university divest itself of its South African securities. Since his school was affiliated with a mainline denomination, indeed bore its name, Greg could not understand how it could resist what was obviously a moral imperative. He also exercised a growing impatience with the church-at-large for its hesitancy to take positions he believed were clearly matters of religious conscience. And yet the church was the place in which he had developed his ethical stance.

Following college, Greg enrolled in a denominational seminary, where he continued his pilgrimage as an intern in an urban working-class congregation. He also spent time in Guatemala and Nicaragua—supported by his home congregation and his denomination. Through it all, however, his anger at the church for its lack of commitment to the things he found important continued to grow. At the ordination service I laid the same charge on him I had privately repeated to him many times during our times together. "Greg, love the church!"

How can one love this great ecclesiastical blunder machine? That was Greg's question for all the years I knew him. It is probably his question today, even as he continues his ministry in an Arkansas congregation.

I could never stand in judgment on him for his strong feelings about ethical issues, since for almost a half a century that has been my question. Given all the things that we have been saying about this socially stratified, irrelevant, lukewarm institution, how can anyone with an ounce of commitment or sense love it?

And yet I do. I love it profoundly. There is even a shadowed sense in which I love it incompletely as Christ loved it fully.

> With his own blood he bought her,
> And for her life he died.
> Samuel Stone

I have not had to shed blood for her, but I have served her and wept for her and over her and given myself in her service. And I intend to continue to do so "till traveling days are o'er." The fights I have had with the church have been lovers' quarrels. Sometimes they have been loud and angry. At one point they almost terminated in divorce.

Perhaps the crisis I confronted along the way was what we now call "ministerial burnout"—although it is hard to see why so many these days who have hardly ever been warm, let alone on fire, should suffer from that disability. There were a number of years in the late '60s and early '70s, when I was operating on the edge—or even sometimes over the edge. As pastor of a congregation on the campus of the University of Chicago during its most radical period, I found myself day and night with highly motivated students who seemed intent on bringing down the administration of the university, if not the government of the nation. I personally shared in sheltering the Chicago eight—later the Chicago seven. I did my best to keep their violence constrained, but I never lost faith in their vision. I was called before the grand jury when the Chicago eight were indicted, and was confronted by two members of our college youth group, who alleged that I was part of the plot. It turned out that these two trusted young men were police informers who had infiltrated the church.

During that same era a gang war had erupted in our neighborhood between two large African-American youth groups. Shootings and knifings were common. I had the difficult task of burying young men from both the Devils Disciples and the Blackstone Rangers. My task was to establish a neutral zone in the church and its surrounding neighborhood, and to attempt some sort of negotiated settlement of their street war. Even if the level of violence did decline slightly, I knew I was being used by both gangs. There are times when being used and knowing it is just part of the deal. I have always wanted to live in a pure world where right and wrong were plain and absolute, but to this point I have never come upon its location.

The church building was the meeting place, lunchroom, coffee house, and general headquarters for both the radical students and the gang members. It was also a safe haven for black youths from the community who didn't want to be caught up in either gang. During these same years I was teaching at Chicago Theological Seminary and doing what I could to pastor a vigorous congregation. Through it all, the congregation was supportive, even at its own peril. One night the church was firebombed. That story is recited elsewhere in this book.

The time came when I knew I had to get out of everything: the church, the seminary, the radical student movement, the city, the gangs, a marriage, friendships. And that is what I did. It had become clear to me that even at its best the church could not and would not share in the revolutionary activity called for if it were to be faithful to the goals of God's coming reign. And so I left.

For almost three years I was the chief operating officer of a Chicago-based educational corporation, and a witness for the Sub-Committee on Post-Secondary Education of the U.S. Congressional Committee on Education and Labor. My son and I lived in an suburban apartment, and when I attended church it was at the safe, serene, nonthreatening Episcopal parish across the street.

While the congregation I attended was a comfortable haven, I had concluded that churches in general were useless in the reformation of society. Their skills lay in comforting the afflicted. If anything for good was to happen in the world at large, the church would have little to do with it, no matter how its ecclesial systems were shaped. And if I was to make any difference, I would be obliged to operate in the business world, educational institutions, and the political systems that ran Chicago. I could not and did not love the church!

It didn't take long for my naiveté to be unmasked. After two years trying to make my way in that milieu, it came to me that despite all its faults, if there was any hope, any authenticity, any institution that could make a difference, it was the church. All the faults one could attribute to the effete mainline church were also well established in every other social structure—and few of the graces. Sinfulness, selfishness, misappropriated energy, lethargy, clannishness, and all the rest were not the sole property of the religious institution. Everything I saw in the secular world seethed with the same diseases—and even worse.

Not in business, politics, radical movements for social reformation, the youth culture, or the academy did I find the dynamic and the grace Christ had given the church. In addition, what else had established branches on street corners in every neighborhood, urban and rural? Where else did ordinary men and women voluntarily give considerable portions of what they owned for the benefit of those they might not even know or ever see, those who would give them nothing in return nor be under any obligation?

Nothing I had found in the secular world generated as much compassion for the left out, the poor, the strangers, and the outsiders. And what else had branch offices all over the world where anyone could be made welcome just by presenting themselves?

It was the church that cared about the bodies and souls of folks regardless of their language, race, or family constellation. In short, while it might have been in mud jars—earthen vessels— it was the church that had heard, responded to, and held the gospel. Nowhere else did I find the lived-out message of grace and love I had experienced in the church.

It was in the church that I was accepted just as I was. It was the church that had held me close when I was injured, sheltered my children, and supported me when my mother and father, my brother, and, later, my son died.

And what is more, when I was still a lad of sixteen, God had laid a hand on my shoulder and called me to be a servant, a minister of that gospel. After I had spent two years in the business world, a congregation in a midwestern city invited me to be their minister. I responded, and for the next eighteen years my life in that place was fulfilled, blessed, and overwhelmed with grace.

It was out of that personal history I was able to say to Greg, "Love the church." I did not even mean the church in some frothy generic form, but rather the traditional middle-class mainline church. The Christian gospel is, at heart, incarnational. God has been and is in our midst in the person we know as Jesus the Christ, and that presence takes shape and is embodied in a living institution called the church. God is not so much revealed in a book or a doctrine as in a people. Apart from anything any of us have done, we have been grafted into that people, and by that grafting know who we are.

Will the church survive? Certainly not as we have known it. Dr. William Tabernee, President of Phillips Graduate Seminary, likens its current status to a train entering a tunnel, knowing that the transit will be dark, and that none of the passengers would have the slightest awareness of what the world will be like when it emerges at the other end.

It may be that God is finished with the church we have known. No institution has the seeds of eternity planted in its fabric, and certainly any institution that believes it does is already under judgment. If God is finished with us, or we have been well used and are now used up, the journey has been worth the effort.

We press forward, toward the goal of the upward call of God in Christ Jesus. Yet our faith does not rest in the church, but in the power and grace of God, to whom be glory forever.

For those of you who have said, "Yes, yes" as you have worked your way through the criticisms in these pages, I say: Love the church, and trust the God who has called it into being. Together with all of creation, stand on tiptoe to see what new thing God is about to do. And pray for the day that will surely come when all things are reconciled to God, things in heaven and things on earth.

Questions for Reflection and Discussion

1. In summing up, how do you understand the major thesis of this book? Do you believe that mainline churches are really facing a number of years in Babylonian captivity? If so, how do you believe they should respond? If not, what do you think the future of mainline denominations might be?

2. You may want to go back over the book, with particular reference to the questions for study at the end of each chapter. If you were going to design a congregation from scratch, what would you do and how would it look when you had completed your project?

3. In what way does your design meet the specific needs of this age? Or are you convinced of the ecclesiastical concept that "one size fits all"?

4. Few of us will design a church from the ground up. We will be forced to work with what we have. The question is, how shall our congregations be re-formed to meet the challenges of the time and place in which they are found?

5. Do you really love the church? If so, how will this influence your commitment in the days ahead?